JUDICIAL TRANSPARENCY AND ETHICS

HEARING

BEFORE THE

SUBCOMMITTEE ON
COURTS, INTELLECTUAL PROPERTY,
AND THE INTERNET

OF THE

COMMITTEE ON THE JUDICIARY
HOUSE OF REPRESENTATIVES

ONE HUNDRED FIFTEENTH CONGRESS

FIRST SESSION

FEBRUARY 14, 2017

Serial No. 115–1

Printed for the use of the Committee on the Judiciary

Available via the World Wide Web: http://judiciary.house.gov

U.S. GOVERNMENT PUBLISHING OFFICE

24–270 PDF   WASHINGTON : 2017

For sale by the Superintendent of Documents, U.S. Government Publishing Office
Internet: bookstore.gpo.gov   Phone: toll free (866) 512–1800; DC area (202) 512–1800
Fax: (202) 512–2104   Mail: Stop IDCC, Washington, DC 20402–0001

COMMITTEE ON THE JUDICIARY

BOB GOODLATTE, Virginia, *Chairman*

F. JAMES SENSENBRENNER, JR., Wisconsin
LAMAR S. SMITH, Texas
STEVE CHABOT, Ohio
DARRELL E. ISSA, California
STEVE KING, Iowa
TRENT FRANKS, Arizona
LOUIE GOHMERT, Texas
JIM JORDAN, Ohio
TED POE, Texas
JASON CHAFFETZ, Utah
TOM MARINO, Pennsylvania
TREY GOWDY, South Carolina
RAUL LABRADOR, Idaho
BLAKE FARENTHOLD, Texas
DOUG COLLINS, Georgia
RON DeSANTIS, Florida
KEN BUCK, Colorado
JOHN RATCLIFFE, Texas
MIKE BISHOP, Michigan
MARTHA ROBY, Alabama
MATT GAETZ, Florida
MIKE JOHNSON, Louisiana
ANDY BIGGS, Arizona

JOHN CONYERS, JR., Michigan, *Ranking Member*
JERROLD NADLER, New York
ZOE LOFGREN, California
SHEILA JACKSON LEE, Texas
STEVE COHEN, Tennessee
HENRY C. "HANK" JOHNSON, JR., Georgia
TED DEUTCH, Florida
LUIS V. GUTIERREZ, Illinois
KAREN BASS, California
CEDRIC RICHMOND, Louisiana
HAKEEM JEFFRIES, New York
DAVID N. CICILLINE, Rhode Island
ERIC SWALWELL, California
TED LIEU, California
JAMIE RASKIN, Maryland
PRAMILA JAYAPAL, Washington
BRADLEY SCHNEIDER, Illinois

SHELLEY HUSBAND, *Chief of Staff & General Counsel*
PERRY APELBAUM, *Minority Staff Director & Chief Counsel*

———

SUBCOMMITTEE ON COURTS, INTELLECTUAL PROPERTY, AND THE INTERNET

DARRELL E. ISSA, California, *Chairman*
DOUG COLLINS, Georgia, *Vice-Chairman*

LAMAR S. SMITH, Texas
STEVE CHABOT, Ohio
TRENT FRANKS, Arizona
JIM JORDAN, Ohio
TED POE, Texas
JASON CHAFFETZ, Utah
TOM MARINO, Pennsylvania
RAUL LABRADOR, Idaho
BLAKE FARENTHOLD, Texas
RON DeSANTIS, Florida
MATT GAETZ, Florida
ANDY BIGGS, Arizona

JERROLD NADLER, New York
HENRY C. "HANK" JOHNSON, JR., Georgia
TED DEUTCH, Florida
KAREN BASS, California
CEDRIC RICHMOND, Louisiana
HAKEEM JEFFRIES, New York
ERIC SWALWELL, California
TED LIEU, California
BRADLEY SCHNEIDER, Illinois
ZOE LOFGREN, California
STEVE COHEN, Tennessee
LUIS V. GUTIERREZ, Illinois

JOE KEELEY, *Chief Counsel*
JASON EVERETT, *Minority Counsel*

(II)

CONTENTS

FEBRUARY 14, 2017

Page

OPENING STATEMENTS

The Honorable Darrell E. Issa, a Representative in Congress from the State of California, and Chairman, Subcommittee on Courts, Intellectual Property, and the Internet 1
The Honorable Jerrold Nadler, a Representative in Congress from the State of New York, and Ranking Member, Subcommittee on Courts, Intellectual Property, and the Internet 2
The Honorable Bob Goodlatte, a Representative in Congress from the State of Virginia, and Chairman, Committee on the Judiciary 4
The Honorable John Conyers, Jr., a Representative in Congress from the State of Michigan, and Ranking Member, Committee on the Judiciary 5

WITNESSES

Mickey H. Osterreicher, Esq., General Counsel, National Press Photographers Association (NPPA)
Oral Testimony 7
Prepared Statement 10
Thomas R. Bruce, Professor, and Director, Legal Information Institute, Cornell University
Oral Testimony 21
Prepared Statement 23
Charles G. Geyh, John F. Kimerling Professor of Law, Indiana Law School
Oral Testimony 31
Prepared Statement 33

LETTERS, STATEMENTS, ETC., SUBMITTED FOR THE HEARING

Material submitted by the Honorable Jerrold Nadler, a Representative in Congress from the State of New York, and Ranking Member, Subcommittee on Courts, Intellectual Property, and the Internet 47

OFFICIAL HEARING RECORD

MATERIAL SUBMITTED FOR THE HEARING RECORD BUT NOT REPRINTED

Material submitted by the Honorable Darrell E. Issa, a Representative in Congress from the State of California, and Chairman, Subcommittee on Courts, Intellectual Property, and the Internet. This submission is available at the Subcommittee and can also be accessed at:

http://docs.house.gov/Committee/Calendar/ByEvent.aspx?EventID=105547

JUDICIAL TRANSPARENCY AND ETHICS

TUESDAY, FEBRUARY 14, 2017

HOUSE OF REPRESENTATIVES

SUBCOMMITTEE ON COURTS, INTELLECTUAL PROPERTY,
AND THE INTERNET

COMMITTEE ON THE JUDICIARY

Washington, DC.

The Subcommittee met, pursuant to call, at 10:06 a.m., in room 2141, Rayburn House Office Building, the Honorable Darrell E. Issa (Chairman of the Subcommittee) presiding.

Present: Representatives Issa, Goodlatte, Chabot, Jordan, Poe, Marino, Labrador, DeSantis, Gaetz, Biggs, Nadler, Conyers, Deutch, Bass, Jeffries, Swalwell, Lieu, Lofgren, Johnson, and Jackson Lee.

Staff Present: (Majority) Joe Keeley, Chief Counsel; Zack Walz, Clerk; and (Minority) Jason Everett, Minority Counsel.

Mr. ISSA. The Subcommittee on Courts, Intellectual Property, and the Internet will come to order with or without a gavel.

Without objection, the Chair is authorized to declare a recess of the Committee at any time.

We welcome everyone here today for a hearing on judicial transparency and ethics. And I now recognize myself for a quick opening statement.

As we all know, there are three branches of government. The first branch has a key responsibility to make laws. Those laws, consistent with the Constitution, include the oversight of the other two branches. No one doubts for one moment that Congress has a responsibility to oversee Article II, the executive branch.

Oddly enough, the courts have given us explicit rulings to just that, the need for oversight, particularly the need to oversight of our appropriation, moneys of the taxpayers. And yet in many, many ways, the court, not just the Supreme Court, but all of the courts, tend to be fairly insular and seem to believe that they and they alone will determine what they and they alone shall do. Up to a point, this Member would agree with them. Agree that, in fact, its interference by the executive branch or by Congress in their deliberative process in how they go about determining what is justice, is in fact, an area that we need not and should not tread upon lightly.

However, when it comes to the taxation of the American people, which includes fees; when it comes to transparency, meaning

American citizens and others' right to know; when it comes to the ethics of the judiciary, we have an obligation. We cannot alone simply say we will wait to impeach a judge from time to time about once every couple of decades. The real question of whether or not judges are operating appropriately in their courtroom, not just ethically but, in fact, since it is a lifetime appointment, often we recognize that judges grow old, judges have personal lives, and in fact, overseeing whether or not that system is properly maintained to ensure that every judge is doing and capable of doing their job when they take the bench.

Additionally, today, we will talk about PACER. Most Americans do not know what PACER is, but by the end of this hearing, they will understand that everything that goes on in a courtroom and then beyond, all the way through the appellate process, is made available to the public through PACER, but not necessarily for free. We all know that fees are paid when you are prosecuting a case and judgments include court cost. What most people don't know is that the court charges 10 cents an electronic page for their records and makes a tidy profit on it, which they use in any way they see fit and, in fact, circumvent appropriations.

That is not to say that everything they spend the money on is inappropriate or that this fund's use to ensure that we expand the ability to keep up with records is in fact inappropriate, but it does beg the question of, should the American people in this day and age receive more information more quickly and less expensively or should we allow the court to set an amount in a vacuum that allows them to use it for areas that are often well outside of their essential needs.

As I mentioned earlier, judges grow old, Alzheimer's is real, aphasia is real, and there is no system that guarantees that a judge in his or her everyday life is, in fact, being properly checked to ensure that they are able to do their job, one of the most important jobs in a democracy.

Today, we will hear about cameras in the courtroom. There will be people on the dais for it and there will be people against it. I will, for one, remain open minded, recognizing that the Chief Jus- tice is adamantly opposed to it but that, in fact, there is a question of whether or not it is his right to preclude that or it is our obliga- tion to protect the Court from becoming much like the House floor. And in each side of that argument, there will be those who speak. I think it is important today that we realize that this is the first of many hearings that will be held on the courts. And during this 2 years, I am dedicated, in addition to the questions of the internet and questions of intellectual property, to reassert this Committee's responsibility to oversee the courts, to help them do their job bet- ter, to be a conduit for what they want and, in fact, an oversight of what they do.

And with that, I would like to recognize the Ranking Member of the Subcommittee, the gentleman from New York, Mr. Nadler, for his opening statement.

Mr. NADLER. Thank you, Mr. Chairman.

Mr. Chairman, the Federal judiciary is the envy of the world. Dedicated to upholding the rule of law, our court system provides a forum for private parties to resolve their disputes peacefully and enable society to punish those who violate the law. It also safe-guards our treasured liberties and ensures that the government stays within constitutional boundaries.

Unfortunately, however, we cannot ignore the fact that the judiciary is under a sustained attack right now, and it is coming from what should be one of the most unlikely of places, the Oval Office. That's right, the President of the United States, whose unconstitutional Muslim ban has been rightly thwarted by the courts, has launched an unprecedented and dangerous campaign to threaten and attempt to delegitimize the judiciary and any judge who would dare enforce limits on his power.

It is not uncommon for Presidents of both parties to speak out against court decisions with which they disagree, but never before have we seen such a brazen attempt by a President to erode public confidence in the courts as fair and neutral arbiters of the law. As most people are aware, after Judge James Robart temporarily blocked enforcement of President Trump's immigration executive order, the President took to Twitter to label him a "so-called judge." This was followed by several other tweets that attacked Judge Robart personally, called his decision political, and even claimed that if something happened to the United States, the judge and the court system should be blamed.

Next, the President turned his target to the Ninth Circuit judges considering the appeal of Judge Robart's order. In his speech the morning after the court's hearing but even before its ruling, Mr. Trump called the proceedings "disgraceful," and "so political," while also claiming that the judges failed to grasp concepts that even "a bad high school student would understand."

Then after the Ninth Circuit left Judge Robart's order in place, one of President Trump's top advisers, Stephen Miller said, "The judiciary is not supreme," and challenged the court's legitimacy to question the President's interpretation of the law.

Finally, the President summed up his thoughts on Twitter this weekend writing "our legal system is broken." I beg to differ. I think our court system worked exactly as it is supposed to. As chaos and confusion reigned at our Nation's airports, the court stepped in to clarify that no one is above the law and that the Constitution still provides certain fundamental protections.

Although the drama surrounding President Trump's executive order has been temporarily set aside, we must not become complacent in the face of such attacks on the integrity and legitimacy of individual judges or the court system generally. Especially when they come from the President of the United States, such attacks are both inappropriate and reckless and dangerous.

Already there have been reports that judges involved in legal challenges to the executive order have been threatened and requiring increased security protection. Moreover, President Trump's broadsides against the Federal courts threaten to undermine public confidence in the institution of the judiciary itself.

An independent judiciary is fundamental to the checks and balances that are embodied in the separation of powers and is essential to maintaining liberty and the rule of law. I am disturbed that the President either does not appreciate the role that an independent judiciary plays in our constitutional system or it does appreciate it and seeks to undermine it. I hope that my Republican colleagues, especially on this Committee, will join me in demanding that the President cease these attacks on the judiciary immediately.

My deep respect for the judiciary does not mean, of course, that there are no improvements that we can make to the court system, particularly when it comes to transparency. This includes stronger ethics and disclosure requirements, particularly with respect to the Supreme Court, which is not bound by the code of ethics that applies to other Federal judges.

Another important transparency measure would be televising judicial proceedings, at least in the appellate courts. I know that the judicial conference has undertaken a pilot project to bring cameras to the courtroom, but I think it is time to expand this across the Federal appellate courts. I recognize there are privacy concerns when it comes to trial court proceedings, but there is no reason to shield the appellate courts from public view. Public scrutiny of governmental proceedings and an informed citizenry is essential to democracy.

Most courts are closed to cameras, effectively putting them off limits to the public at large. Transcripts and audio recordings, some of which are made public days or in some weeks, even weeks later, are poor substitutes for the immediate visual experience. That is why yesterday I reintroduced the bipartisan Eyes on the Courts Act. This legislation would finally bring important cases into public view by requiring that cameras be allowed in all Supreme Court and Federal appellate court proceedings.

I do not share the concerns of those who believe that the highly trained lawyers and judges in appellate court proceedings tackling some of the most important issues facing our country will start playing to the cameras, nor am I aware of any such problems occurring in those Federal courts where cameras have been used.

The Nation was riveted by the live audio stream of the Ninth Circuit's consideration of the President's executive order last week. Clearly, there is great interest in wider access to court proceedings, and I see no reason the public should be prevented from witnessing the other important cases considered in the Federal appellate courts.

I respect the difficulty and important job that the Federal judiciary performs. If my bill becomes law, the public will have an opportunity to watch them in action and to gain a greater understanding and appreciation of their critical work.

I look forward to hearing from our witnesses on this issue and the other important topics affecting the Federal judiciary. And I yield back the balance of my time.

Mr. ISSA. I thank the gentleman.

We now recognize the Chairman of the full Committee, the gentleman from Virginia, Mr. Goodlatte, for his opening statement.

Mr. GOODLATTE. Thank you, Mr. Chairman.

This morning, the Judiciary Committee continues its examination of our Nation's—I have a brief delay here. Excuse me.

This morning, the Judiciary Committee continues its examination of our Nation's Federal judicial system. It is widely recognized that the trust that the American people have in our court system is crucial to its success. While this trust has been cultivated over many generations, it can be quickly lost. This is why it is important that the judiciary continue to operate in a transparent manner at all times and handle the disputes before it efficiently, ethically, and impartially.

This morning, we will hear from three witnesses who will present their ideas regarding ways to increase judicial transparency and accountability. These suggestions include greater use of audio and video recordings in courtrooms, free or lower cost access to court documents through the PACER system or potential replacements for it, and public disclosure of recusal decisions.

Other issues we will consider today are the judicial disability and disciplinary processes. Decisions made by judges with undiagnosed medical conditions can be subject to challenge years later. It is crucial that all judges have the resources and confidential programs needed to assist them if they have any questions about their fitness to serve.

Regarding judicial discipline, there have been relatively few impeachments of Federal judges by the House of Representatives. The Federal judiciary has its own internal disciplinary system that, in theory, addresses misconduct before the conduct escalates to the level where impeachment would be warranted. However, many Members of Congress have questions about the judiciary's disciplinary system.

Today, we will explore this system further, including examining the remedies available for judicial misconduct, their application, and the constitutional and other limitations on those remedies.

I want to thank our witnesses for making time available to be here in order to provide testimony for improving our Nation's judiciary.

Mr. Chairman, I yield back.

Mr. ISSA. I thank the gentleman. It is now my pleasure to recognize the gentleman from Michigan, Mr. Conyers, for his opening statement.

Mr. CONYERS. Thank you, Chairman Issa.

Welcome to all our witnesses.

Today's hearing gives us an important opportunity to examine judicial transparency and ethics issues, but I would like to begin my remarks by addressing some of the troubling statements President Trump has made about judges and the judiciary.

Earlier this month, the President disparagingly referred to a member of the Federal bench as a so-called judge and criticized his decision as ridiculous. This judge is now in receipt of death threats.

Last year, while campaigning for the Presidency, he called into question the validity of a ruling by a Federal judge because of the judge's ethnic background.

Most recently, President Trump, in opposing a decision rendered by the Ninth Circuit, said even a bad high school student could understand that his immigration ban was authorized by law and that it was a political decision.

President Trump's personal attacks against individual judges as well as disrespectful comments regarding the Federal judiciary as a whole threatened the fundamental principles of our constitutional form of government, namely respect for the rule of law and an independent judiciary. Even his Supreme Court nominee, Neil Gorsuch, characterized President Trump's comments about the judiciary as disheartening and demoralizing.

Respect for the Federal judiciary should be a nonpartisan issue, and this hearing is an example, an excellent example, I might add, of cooperation with respect to oversight of that branch. Yet we must also be mindful of the potentially destructive attacks against the Federal judiciary, even if those attacks emanate from the executive office of the President.

Accordingly, I hope my friends on the other side of the aisle will join me today in condemning President Trump's comments threatening the legitimacy of our judicial branch and efforts to cast aspersions against individual Federal judges.

An independent judiciary is critical, of course, to our Nation's constitutional system of checks and balances, and we should do everything possible to ensure that that system is not undermined.

As to the additional areas that we will consider today, I do support having cameras in the courtroom, but continue to believe their impact must be more carefully considered. The Judicial Conference, for example, notes that cameras in the courtroom could potentially impair the fundamental right of a citizen to a fair and impartial trial, and Justice Elena Kagan warns that televised coverage of Federal court proceedings would encourage participants to play to the camera.

I would like to hear proponents of cameras in the courtroom explain how those efforts will neither undermine a citizen's right to due process and a fair trial, nor have a material effect on an individual's willingness to testify out of fear of being a target for retribution or intimidation.

Finally, I support increased transparency of the judiciary. Last week, the Ninth Circuit Court of Appeals provided live-stream coverage of the oral argument on the Administration's appeal of the lower court's imposition of a nationwide stay of President Trump's immigration order. Efforts such as these by the Federal judiciary, which makes their processes more readily available to the public, will promote even greater respect and understanding of the Federal court system and the rule of law. And as we promote transparency, we must also be mindful of the need to ensure the safety and security of our judges, law enforcement officers, and others participating in the judicial process.

I thank and applaud the Chairman for holding this hearing. And I yield back the balance of my time.

Mr. ISSA. I thank the gentleman.

I now—without objection, other Members' opening statements will be made in the record.

Today we have a distinguished panel of witnesses whose written statements have been entered into the record. And without objection, all your written statements and extraneous material will be admitted into the record.

Without objection, so ordered.

But today, I would ask that you summarize your opening statements in about 5 minutes. To help you stay within the timing, you know the lights, you have all been here before, please, green means go, yellow means you got a minute, and red means you will get a ticket if you run the light.

Before introducing our witnesses, it is the rule of the Committee that all witnesses be sworn. So I would ask that you please rise to take the oath and raise your right hands.

Do you solemnly swear or affirm that the testimony you are about to give will be the truth, the whole truth, and nothing but the truth.

Please be seated.

Let the record indicate that all witnesses answered in the affirmative.

Our witnesses today include Mr. Mickey Osterreicher.

Mr. OSTERREICHER. Osterreicher.

Mr. ISSA. Osterreicher. More importantly, the general counsel for the National Press Photographers Association, who needless to say have been giving us images of the courts for, more or less, a century. Professor Thomas Bruce is the cofounder and director of the Legal Information Institute at Cornell University. Welcome. And Professor Charles Geyh is professor at Indiana University—your, what is it, Maurer——

Mr. GEYH. Maurer.

Mr. ISSA.—School of Law. And each comes with a level of expertise to help guide us through three different areas that we are going to look at today. So welcome.

You are recognized for 5 minutes.

TESTIMONY OF MICKEY H. OSTERREICHER, ESQ., GENERAL COUNSEL, NATIONAL PRESS PHOTOGRAPHERS ASSOCIATION (NPPA)

Mr. OSTERREICHER. Chairman Issa, Ranking Member Conyers, Ranking Member Nadler, and other Members of the Subcommittee, good morning, and thank you for the opportunity to appear here today.

My name is Mickey Osterreicher. I am of counsel to the law firm of Barclay & Damon, and I am here today in my capacity as general counsel for the National Press Photographers Association, an organization which was founded in 1946 and of which I have been a member since 1973.

As the voice of visual journalists, the NPPA vigorously promotes and defends the rights of photographers and journalists, including intellectual property rights and freedom of speech in all its forms, especially as it relates to visual journalism.

By way of background, I am an award-winning visual journalist with over 40 years experience in print and broadcast. During that career, I have covered hundreds of court cases from the Attica trials to the murder trial of O.J. Simpson. I was actively involved in the New York State experiment between 1987 and 1997 entitled, "Electronic Coverage of Judicial Proceedings." And by electronic, I mean audiovisual recordings, still photography, broadcasting, televising, or internet streaming both in realtime or hyperlinked replay.

In an era of fake news and alternative facts, there is no better way to ensure transparency and promote confidence in the fair administration of justice than to expand electronic coverage of Federal court proceedings. Transparent court proceedings improve the quality of testimony, persuade unknown witnesses to come forward, make trial participants more conscientious, and provide the opportunity to better observe the workings of our judicial system. To foster that essential principle, almost every State allows electronic coverage of criminal, civil, and appellate proceedings, to some degree.

For many years, Congress has proposed legislation to allow such coverage, most recently by Representative Connolly and Judge Poe. Representative Nadler also introduced a bill in 2015, which he just reintroduced. The NPPA commends and supports these ongoing efforts.

More recently, there have been some advances and some lost opportunities in this area. For example, the Ninth Circuit began livestreaming audio of oral arguments in 2015, and the Second Circuit continues its policy of permitting electronic coverage for cases with heightened interest. By comparison, the Supreme Court has released same-day audio of an oral argument only once, despite numerous requests to do so. In 2015, it denied such a petition for two of the year's most important cases.

The last Federal cameras pilot program officially ended in 2015, and while the judicial conference voted against expanding or continuing that project, it did permit three of the participating trial court programs in the Ninth Circuit to remain operational. Just this month, electronic coverage was allowed in the *State of Washington v. Trump*, which was recorded and uploaded to the court's website.

Last week, the telephonic arguments of the appeal in that case were heard live with approximately 137,000 connections to the audio stream from the court's YouTube site. CNN, which also broadcast the arguments, averaged 1.5 million total viewers during that hour. Millions more may have tuned in on cable news outlets, local news stations, and countless other news websites.

These latest developments weigh strongly in favor of electronic coverage and should also prompt the Judicial Conference, along with the High Court itself, to finally promulgate common-sense guidelines, permanently allowing such access through the Federal court system, up to and including the U.S. Supreme Court.

Justice Stewart noted in 1965, we move in an area touching the realm of free communication, and for that reason, if nor no other, I would be wary of any—of imposing any, per se, rule, which, in light of future technology, may serve to stifle or abridge true First Amendment rights.

The Framers envisioned court as being part of a public square, a place in a merging —in an emerging Nation where anyone could stop in to observe the proceedings and be assured of the integrity of our system of justice. Given the increasing complexity of our society and the size of our communities, that aspiration is exceedingly more difficult to achieve. As Chief Justice Burger stated in a 1980 case, people in an open society do not demand infallibility from their institutions, but it is difficult for them to accept what they are prohibited from observing.

The ability of the public to view actual courtroom proceedings should not be trivialized. It touches on an important right, which goes well beyond the mere satisfaction of viewer curiosity. And that right, advanced by electronic coverage, is the right of the people to monitor the official functions of their government, including that of the judiciary. Nothing is more fundamental to our democratic system of governance.

The NPPA looks forward to working with you on these issues and thanks you for the opportunity to testify. I welcome your questions.

[The prepared statement of Mr. Osterreicher follows:]

BEFORE THE
HOUSE OF REPRESENTATIVES COMMITTEE ON THE JUDICIARY
SUBCOMMITTEE ON COURTS, IP AND THE INTERNET

WASHINGTON, D.C.

HEARING ON
JUDICIAL TRANSPARENCY AND ETHICS

TESTIMONY OF THE
NATIONAL PRESS PHOTOGRAPHERS ASSOCIATION (NPPA)

MICKEY H. OSTERREICHER, GENERAL COUNSEL
NATIONAL PRESS PHOTOGRAPHERS ASSOCIATION

120 HOOPER ROAD
ATHENS, GA 3062
716.983.7800
LAWYER@NPPA.ORG

February 14, 2017

Subcommittee on Courts, Intellectual Property and the Internet

Committee on the Judiciary
United States House of Representatives
115th Congress, 1st Session

Hearing On
Judicial Transparency and Ethics

Testimony of Mickey H. Osterreicher
General Counsel, National Press Photographers Association (NPPA)

February 14, 2017

Committee Chairman Goodlatte, Committee Ranking Member Conyers, Subcommittee Chairman Issa, Vice Chairman Collins, Subcommittee Ranking Member Nadler and other members of the subcommittee, good morning and thank you for the opportunity to appear before you to discuss electronic coverage of federal court proceedings as it pertains to judicial transparency and ethics.

Background

My name is Mickey Osterreicher. I am of counsel to the law firm of Barclay & Damon LLP in its Media & First Amendment Law Practice Area in Buffalo, N.Y., and appear here today in my capacity as general counsel for the National Press Photographers Association ("NPPA"), an organization which was founded in 1946 and of which I have been a member since 1973.

As the "Voice of Visual Journalists" the NPPA is a 501(c)(6) non-profit organization dedicated to the advancement of visual journalism in its creation, editing and distribution. Our approximately 6,000 members include television and still photographers, editors, students and representatives of businesses that serve the visual journalism community. Since its founding, the NPPA has vigorously promoted and defended the rights of photographers and journalists, including intellectual property rights and freedom of the press in all its forms, especially as it relates to visual journalism.

Additionally, the NPPA is one of 20 legal and media organizations that are members of the Coalition for Court Transparency, a national non-partisan alliance that advocates for greater openness and transparency from the federal court system, including the U.S. Supreme Court.

By way of background, I am an award-winning visual journalist with over forty years' experience in print and broadcast. My work has appeared in such publications as the New York Times, Time, Newsweek and USA Today as well as on ABC World News Tonight, Nightline, Good Morning America, NBC Nightly News and ESPN.

During that career, I have covered hundreds of court cases from the Attica trials to the murder trial of O.J. Simpson. I was actively involved in the 10-year experiment (1987 -1997) under New York Judicial Law § 218, entitled "Electronic Coverage of Judicial Proceedings"[1] (such "electronic coverage" hereinafter referring to: audio-visual recordings, still photography, broadcasting, televising, or Internet streaming (real-time or hyperlinked replay)).

Electronic Coverage in Federal Courts

In a time of "fake news" and "alternative facts" there is no better way to ensure transparency and promote confidence in the fair administration of justice than to expand electronic coverage of federal court proceedings. The Sixth Amendment guarantees "the right to a speedy and public trial" and since the time that amendment was adopted, our history makes clear that openness in court proceedings improves the quality of testimony, persuades unknown witnesses to come forward, makes trial participants more conscientious and generally provides the American public the opportunity to

---

[1] *See* http://codes.lp.findlaw.com/nycode/JUD/7-A/218

better observe the workings of our judicial system. To foster that essential transparency, almost every state allows electronic coverage of criminal, civil and appellate proceedings to some degree.

In December 2014, I had the opportunity to testify[2] before this subcommittee in support of H.R.917 – "Sunshine in the Courtroom Act of 2015." Last month Representatives Gerry Connolly (D-VA) and Judge Ted Poe (R-TX)[3] reintroduced H.R. 464 – "The Cameras in the Court Act,"[4] which would help ensure transparency and accountability in the judicial branch by "permitting the televising of Supreme Court proceedings."[5] If passed the measure would amend 28 U.S.C. 45 by adding language contained in Section 678 entitled "Televising Supreme Court proceedings," which states: "The Supreme Court shall permit television coverage of all open sessions of the Court unless the Court decides, by a vote of the majority of justices, that allowing such coverage in a particular case would constitute a violation of the due process rights of one or more of the parties before the Court."[6]

In 2015, Rep. Nadler (D-NY) along with Representatives Connolly, Poe and Mike Quigley (D-IL) introduced H.R. 3723 – "Eyes on the Courts Act of 2015" "to provide for media coverage of federal appellate court proceedings, and for other purposes." Hopefully they too will reintroduce that bill. The NPPA commends and supports these ongoing efforts.

During the last few years there have been some advances, and some lost opportunities in the expansion of electronic coverage in federal court. For example, the Ninth Circuit, which in 2003 was the first federal appeals court to post audio of its hearings, began live-streaming audio of oral arguments in January 2015. The Second Circuit continues its policy of permitting electronic recording

---

[2] *See* https://judiciary.house.gov/wp-content/uploads/2016/02/Corrected-120314-Testimony-H.R.-917-Osterreicher.pdf
[3] Connolly and Poe Push for Cameras in the Court, January 12, 2017
https://connolly.house.gov/news/documentsingle.aspx?DocumentID=837
[4] *See* https://www.congress.gov/bill/115th-congress/house-bill/464/text?q=%7B%22search%22%3A%5B%22cameras%22%5D%7D&r=1
[5] *Id.*
[6] *Id.*

for cases with heightened interest, most recently allowing C-SPAN to record and broadcast a January 2015 hearing following remand after the Supreme Court's decision in *Burwell v. Hobby Lobby*.[7] Approximately fifteen (15) Second Circuit cases have been recorded since the end of the first federal cameras pilot program (1991-1994), in which the Second and Ninth Circuits participated along with four district courts.

By comparison, the Supreme Court has released the audio of an oral argument on the same day on which the argument occurred only once, despite numerous requests from media organizations and pro-transparency groups. In February 2015, when a dozen media and pro-transparency groups petitioned the high court for same-day audio for two of the year's most closely-watched cases – *Whole Women's Health v. Hellerstedt*[8] and *U.S. v. Texas*,[9] the Court denied the request, tersely stating, "The court will follow its usual practices regarding the posting of the audio for these arguments" – that being, posting the audio the Friday after the cases are argued. As the Committee is, I am sure aware, late Friday releases are the least effective time to bring important news to the public as people get ready for the weekend.

The most recent federal cameras-in-courts pilot program, (comprised of 14 federal trial courts throughout the country), officially ended on July 18, 2015. In March 2016, the Judicial Conference of the United States voted against expanding or continuing that program, although it did permit three of the participating trial courts in the Ninth Circuit – the Western District of Washington, Northern

---

[7] 573 U.S. ___ (2014)
[8] 579 U.S. ___ (2016)
[9] 579 U.S. ___ (2016)

District of California and District of Guam – to keep their cameras rolling at the court's discretion. To date only six proceedings have been recorded.[10]

During the 2011-2015 pilot program, only about ten percent (10%), of the more than 1,500 proceedings in which the parties were notified of the opportunity to record, resulted in a recording; and less than one-third (1/3) of the nearly 200 judges in pilot courts volunteered to participate in the program.[11]

In April 2016, the U.S. Government Accountability Office (GAO) released a report on "Policies and Perspectives on Video and Audio Coverage of Appellate Court Proceedings."[12] Requested by Senators Dick Durbin and Chuck Grassley along with Rep. Mike Quigley, the report details how state appellate courts and those in other countries handle the issue of electronic coverage. Nearly every appellate judge and attorney interviewed by GAO stated that such coverage enhances public understanding of the courts and offers countless educational opportunities for its citizens, including law students and legal practitioners looking to learn from the those at the pinnacle of their profession.

The GAO report also provided recommendations for improving guidelines for successful electronic coverage of court proceedings. For example, the Florida Supreme Court partners with a local public television station which uses its own equipment to record and live-stream audio and video,

---

[10] Administrative Office of U.S. Courts webpage "Available Court Videos," http://www.uscourts.gov/about-federal-courts/cameras-courts (retrieved Feb. 12, 2017)
[11] "Report of the Judicial Conference Committee on Court Administration and Case Management: Cameras Pilot Program," March 2016, available at http://pdfserver.amlaw.com/nlj/Cameras%20pilot%20project%20committee%20report.pdf
[12] *See* http://www.gao.gov/products/GAO-16-437

while the Ninth Circuit operates its own remote-controlled, unobtrusive cameras and posts videos of hearings to YouTube.[13]

On Nov. 4, 2016, the U.S. Supreme Court live-streamed electronic coverage of a Supreme Court Bar meeting commemorating the life of Justice Antonin Scalia that took place in the building's Great Hall. Immediately following that service, a special session of the Court further honoring the late Justice took place. The Court permitted audio of that session to be live-streamed as well, establishing two High Court firsts on the same day. Most recently, the Supreme Court was asked to permit same-day audio of the oral arguments in *Lee v. Tam*[14] and *Ashcroft v. Abbasi.*[15] That request was made by Fix the Court and was accompanied by signatures from nearly 1,000 people from all 50 states.[16] Unfortunately, the Court once again denied that request.[17]

On Dec. 6, 2016, the Eleventh Circuit Court of Appeals announced that by April 1, 2017, it would begin posting audio recordings of oral argument online. This leaves the Tenth Circuit as the only federal appeals court not to post online audio, thus requiring parties to file a motion to obtain such recordings. Last month the Third Circuit announced it will video-record some oral arguments and post them online a day or so later. Two such cases have already been recorded and posted.[18]

Just this month, two cases in the Ninth Circuit were widely broadcast to much acclaim. The U.S. District Court for the Western District of Washington permitted electronic coverage of the hearing regarding President Trump's temporary travel ban in *State of Washington v. Trump.* That proceeding

---

[13] *See* https://www.youtube.com/user/9thcirc
[14] Docket Number 15-1293
[15] Docket Number 15-1359

[16] *See* http://fixthecourt.com/2017/01/fix-the-court-delivers-petition-to-supreme-court-from-citizens-from-50-states-calling-on-justices-to-release-same-day-audio-in-upcoming-cases/
[17] *See* http://www.multichannel.com/news/courts/supreme-court-denies-same-day-audio-request/410011
[18] *See* http://fixthecourt.com/2016/12/eleventh-circuit-agrees-to-post-oral-argument-audio-online/

was recorded and uploaded to the court's website. Last week, the telephonic arguments of the appeal in that case before a three-judge panel of the Ninth Circuit, were heard live. According to David Madden, Assistant Circuit Executive for the Ninth Circuit U.S. Court of Appeals, "there were approximately 137,000 connections to the live audio stream from the court's YouTube site."[19] "The Situation Room with Wolf Blitzer on CNN averaged 1.5 million total viewers and 490 thousand in the 25-54 demo[graphic] in the 6 p.m. ET hour during the 9th Circuit Court audio hearings," according to an email from Richard Hudock, Public Relations Manager at the CNN Washington bureau. Millions more may have tuned in on cable news outlets, local news stations and countless other news websites.

These latest developments weigh strongly in favor of electronic coverage and should also prompt the Judicial Conference along with the High Court itself to finally promulgate commonsense guidelines permitting such coverage throughout the federal court system, up to and including the U.S. Supreme Court.

Openness and Electronic Coverage of Court Proceedings

Aside from the audio-visual information provided by electronic coverage of court proceedings is the constitutional principle that courts are meant to be "open." It is instructive to remember the words of Justice Stewart in his dissent in *Estes v Texas*[20] (the 1965 Supreme Court case dealing with the televising and broadcasting of a trial) where he admonished that "it is important to remember that we move in an area touching the realm of free communication, and for that reason, if for no other, *I would be wary of imposing any per se rule which, in the light of future technology, might serve to stifle or abridge true First Amendment rights.*"[21]

---

[19] Feb. 7, 2017 Tweet
[20] *Estes v. Texas*, 381 U.S. 532 (1965).
[21] *Id.* at 603-04 (Stewart, J., dissenting) (emphasis added).

The Supreme Court also has recognized a rebuttable presumption of openness and transparency in general when it comes to court proceedings. In *Richmond Newspapers, Inc. v. Virginia*[22] the Court held that under the First Amendment the public, including the press, had a right of access to a criminal trial, because such proceedings had traditionally been open to the public. "What is significant for present purposes is that throughout its evolution, the trial has been open to all who care to observe,"[23] Chief Justice Burger wrote in the plurality opinion.

In 2017 such information on matters of public concern come from broadcast television (including cable) and the Internet (including social media and electronic material on websites provided by once traditional print media). Thus, the ability of the press to disseminate information via electronic coverage of court proceedings is a critical component in affording the public the modern equivalent of attending and observing. As Chief Justice Burger further explained, "people in an open society do not demand infallibility from their institutions, but it is difficult for them to accept what they are prohibited from observing."[24] Justice Stewart, concurring in the judgment, wrote that "the right to speak implies a freedom to listen," and that "the right to publish implies a freedom to gather information."[25] Similarly, I would offer that the right to broadcast implies a similar freedom regarding electronic coverage of federal courtroom proceedings.

The Framers envisioned court as being part of the public square, a place in an emerging nation where anyone could stop in to observe the proceedings and be assured of the integrity of our system of justice. Given the increasing complexity of our society and the size of our communities, that aspiration is exceedingly more difficult. But the core need for openness and transparency is now more crucial

---

[22] *Richmond Newspapers, Inc. v. Virginia*, 448 U.S. 555 (1980).
[23] *Id.* at 564 (plurality opinion of Burger, C.J.).
[24] *Id.* at 572.
[25] *Id.* at 599 (Stewart, J., concurring in the judgment, *citing Branzburg v. Hayes*, 408 U.S. 665, 681).

than ever with accusations of the media reporting "fake news" and government purporting "alternative facts." For citizens, there is no better way to more truthfully relay courtroom proceedings than through the direct and unfiltered lens of electronic coverage to be viewed and heard at home, at work or on the go.

The ability of the public to view actual courtroom proceedings should not be trivialized. It touches on an important right, which goes well beyond the mere satisfaction of viewer curiosity. That right, advanced by electronic coverage, is the right of the people to monitor the official functions of their government, including that of the judicial system. Nothing is more fundamental to our democratic system of governance than the right of the people to know how their government is functioning on their behalf.

Conclusion

The benefits of allowing such electronic coverage are numerous and significant: it will bring transparency to the federal judicial system, provide increased accountability from litigants, judges, and the press, and educate citizens about the judicial process. Electronic coverage will allow the public to ensure that proceedings are conducted fairly, and, by extension, that government system of checks and balances are working correctly. We expect that the watchful eye of the public will demand increased accountability from all courtroom actors, each of whom may feel an increased responsibility to conduct themselves in a manner appropriate to their role, thereby diminishing the risk of rogue actors and other wayward governmental actions potentially harmful to the interests of justice. The press, for its part, will also feel the weight of increased accountability, as it will no longer be the only source of information about the courts, and claims of false, sensationalistic or inaccurate reporting will be readily verifiable by citizens able to view the underlying proceedings for themselves.

More than a half century ago Justice Harlan predicted that "the day may come when television will have become so commonplace an affair in the daily life of the average person as to dissipate all reasonable likelihood that its use in courtrooms may disparage the judicial process."[26] That day has not only come but long since passed into a digital age of instant information.

It cannot be overstated that in this current political climate, when democratic principles are being tested and long-established forms of journalism and mass communications are being questioned, opening courts to electronic coverage is an essential and directly deliverable medium for providing the public with the ability to see and hear that justice is being done; renewing confidence in governmental integrity; and creating improved transparency as to how decisions are made at all steps in the judicial process, especially in the Supreme Court.

We look forward to working with this Subcommittee and the full Judiciary Committee in addressing the issue of electronic coverage of federal court proceedings as it pertains to judicial transparency and ethics.

Thank you for the opportunity to testify. I look forward to answering your questions.

Respectfully submitted,

Mickey H. Osterreicher

Mickey H. Osterreicher, General Counsel

National Press Photographers Association
120 Hooper Street
Athens, GA 30602-3018
lawyer@nppa.org

---

[26] *Estes* at 595-596.

Mr. ISSA. Thank you.
Professor Bruce.

TESTIMONY OF THOMAS R. BRUCE, PROFESSOR, AND DIRECTOR, LEGAL INFORMATION INSTITUTE, CORNELL UNIVERSITY

Mr. BRUCE. Chairman Issa, Ranking Member Conyers, Ranking Member——

Mr. ISSA. If you could pull the mike slightly closer, I would appreciate it.

Mr. BRUCE. Sure.

Mr. ISSA. Thank you.

Mr. BRUCE. Chairman Issa, Ranking Member Nadler, Ranking Member Conyers, Members of the Committee, thank you for inviting me to appear before you today.

My name is Tom Bruce. I am the Director of the Legal Information Institute at Cornell. We have been putting legal information online for the public for 25 years and currently reach an audience of approximately 32 million individuals each year.

I am here to talk to you today about the operation and future direction of the PACER system for public access to the opinions of the Federal courts.

Let me begin with three things that define PACER: First, PACER charges fees for access to public records. That has been the cause of a great deal of criticism, not only because fees erect a barrier for many, but because the revenue from fees at current levels considerably exceeds the cost of operating the system. That is inconsistent with policies established by the Congress in the E-Government Act of 2002.

Second, PACER's technology has struggled to stay up to date. That was, to some extent, an accident of history. PACER was implemented shortly before the introduction of the worldwide web, and it was all too quickly seen as outmoded and out of touch with current technology. Over the last few years, it has made up some of the gap, but the system still falls short on a number of dimensions, notably in the area of search and retrieval.

Third and most important, PACER suffers from a split personality. On the one hand, it is an electronic filing and case management system that supports the Federal courts with an audience of lawyers, judges, and court administrative personnel. On the other, and most important to the public and the Congress, it is a data publishing system that offers the work of the Federal courts to a very wide range of people, including litigants, researchers, and government itself.

Equally, there are a number of things that PACER is not. First, PACER is not transparent in its business model or operations.

Second, PACER is not an adequate facility for research on the activities of the Federal courts. That is chiefly because it does not provide bulk access to its data. Significantly, research activities that might be carried out on behalf of the Congress are impeded. Social Security cases, prisoner appeals, and immigration matters are all examples of areas in which study of judicial outcomes is important to those who have responsibility for investigation and evaluation of operations across the full breadth of the government.

Third, PACER is not an effective protector of privacy. And finally, it is not an adequate vehicle for citable legal research because it lacks a system of unique identifiers.

These are hard problems, especially given the scale and diversity of what is published in PACER, but they are soluble, provided that Congress acts. Both the Congress and the Federal courts have strongly and repeatedly announced their commitment to providing full access, even to unpublished opinions, at minimal or no cost.

So what needs to be done? First, fees need to be removed as quickly as possible. Dissemination fees have strongly inhibited beneficial uses of the data contained in the primary record of the workings of our Federal courts. Consideration should be givento removing per-page viewing fees, or at the very least, paring them back to a level that more closely matches PACER's cost of operation.

Second, the details of PACER's operations and business model need to be far more visible to the Congress and to the public. A CRS report describing the business and technical operation of the system in detail would be more than helpful and would bring welcome clarity to many of the issues involved.

Third, the users of PACER's data publication services need representation in the planning and design processes. Published articles by PACER's designers celebrate the responsiveness of its design to the needs of users of the e-filing and case management systems. That can be charitably interpreted as a sound effort to respond to a range of important customers who are in a position to express their needs to the designers. Understandably, those to whom the designers answer are preoccupied with the e-filing and case management portions of the system and are not nearly as concerned with publication.

Fourth, PACER's data publishing operation should move to a new home. Why not put responsibility for data publishing operations with an organization that has publishing as its primary mission? The Government Publishing Office and the AO already have a pilot program for the publication of judicial opinions underway. It has been successful. It appears to be scalable to the dimensions that PACER would require.

Much work would still be needed. GPO's system only extends right now to about 100 courts. Its chronological range is narrow, and better metadata is needed even within PACER itself.

But the potential benefits are many. First and foremost will be the removal of barriers that prevent the public from exercising the right to know the laws that govern them. Publication systems that permit research utilizing the full range of data available from PACER will make it easier for the Congress to fulfill its responsibilities, improve the efficiency and functioning of the judiciary, and stimulate new approaches to legal information, while encouraging new and innovative businesses.

Thank you for the opportunity to testify today. I look forward to your questions.

[The prepared statement of Mr. Bruce follows:]

Testimony of
Thomas R. Bruce

Co-Founder and Director of the Legal Information Institute
A Research and Publication Activity of the Cornell Law School

before the
House Committee on the
Judiciary's Subcommittee on Courts,
Intellectual Property and the Internet

on
Judicial Transparency and Ethics

February 14, 2017

Comments of the Cornell Legal Information Institute
before the
House Judiciary Committee
Subcommittee on Courts and Intellectual Property

February 14, 2017

Chairman Issa, Ranking Member Nadler, and members of the Committee, thank you for inviting me to appear before you today.

My name is Tom Bruce, and I am the co-founder and Director of the Legal Information Institute, a research, engineering, and publishing activity of the Cornell Law School. In 1992, we were the first to make judicial opinions available via the Web; our publication of the decisions of the Supreme Court anticipated the development of their Web site by 8 years. In the intervening quarter-century, we have gained a great deal of expertise in the creation of advanced technologies for legal publishing, some of it in collaboration with groups well-known to this Committee. We have undertaken joint studies with the Government Publication Office, and consulted on advanced legislative metadata models for the Library of Congress. We served on the House Bulk Data Task Force and as members of the steering committee for its annual Legislative Data Transparency Workshop. Perhaps surprisingly, we have never published materials that are taken from PACER, though we are well-acquainted with its use by others. Last year, the LII's web site at law.cornell.edu provided legal information to more than 32 million unique individuals.

I am here to speak to you about only one of the several important matters before the Committee today, namely the operation and future direction of the PACER system for public access to the opinions of the Federal courts. This is not the first time that this matter has come before the committee, and I intend to be brief. I will not revisit the many criticisms of the capabilities of that system, or of its fee structure, beyond the bare minimum necessary to get a glimpse of a useful way forward.

What PACER is

With that in mind, let me focus on three things that define PACER:

First, PACER charges fees for access to public records. That has been the cause of a great deal of criticism[1], not only because fees erect a barrier for many, but because the revenue from fees at current levels considerably exceeds the cost of operating the system. The excess revenue is diverted for use on

---

[1] Many have taken issue with the charging of fees, and particularly fees beyond cost recovery. See, for example, https://blog.law.cornell.edu/voxpop/2011/02/03/pacer-recap-and-the-movement-to-free-american-case-law/, for an article by Steven Schultze describing the inception of the RECAP project. Wikipedia provides a good list of sources in its treatment of the system, at https://en.wikipedia.org/wiki/PACER_(law), including an article from the New York Times that describes PACER as "cumbersome, arcane, and not free". The Free Law Project's "Downloading Important Cases on PACER Costs More Than A Brand New Car" uses a whimsical method to describe the problem in very concrete terms, comparing the cost of PACER research in a major case to the cost of a Honda Civic. See https://free.law/2016/11/17/downloading-important-cases-on-pacer-costs-more-than-a-brand-new-car/

The fee schedule is currently the object of a class-action lawsuit initiated by three non-profit organizations. See Barry, Kyle. "Alliance for Justice sues the Administrative Office of the U.S. Courts for charging excessive and illegal fees to access court records". Alliance for Justice. (at http://www.afj.org/press-room/press-releases/alliance-for-justice-sues-the-administrative-office-of-the-u-s-courts-for-charging-excessive-and-illegal-fees-to-access-court-records) (retrieved February 10, 2016).

other projects. That is unjustifiable and inconsistent with the policies established by the Congress in the E-Government Act of 2002. [2]

The fee issue is compelling, but it is not the only issue. Dropping fees altogether would be laudable, in that it would remove the economic barriers to public access. It would not relieve other problems, notably with outdated technology[3] and with usable citation – and indeed it might require that the Administrative Office address long-neglected problems with personally-identifiable information in the database.

Second, PACER became outmoded two years after it was built, and in some ways has never caught up. That was, to some extent, an accident of history. Implemented only two years before the introduction of the World-Wide Web created a revolution of rising expectations for online information systems, it was all too quickly seen as outmoded and out of touch with current technology. Unfortunately, improvements came slowly and the gap widened. Recent progress has been more rapid, but the system still falls short on a number of dimensions, notably in the area of search and retrieval[4].

In 1990, there was very little expertise in the design and operation of large-scale case-management and legal-publishing systems outside the two largest commercial legal-information services (recall that this was a time when the Justice Department was, at high cost, buying back its own work product from what was then the West Publishing Company[5], now a division of the Canadian company Thomson-Reuters, much as the government continues to buy its own work back from PACER today). In 2017 the situation is radically different. Expertise is much more widespread, diffused across multiple companies, non-profits, and academic institutions. Legal-publishing and case-management companies are numerous and there is vigorous competition both for market share and for technological advantage[6] at all price points. That is a market that would get further stimulus from a more open PACER.

Innovative approaches are also flowing from the non-profit sector and from government. The Free Law Project[7], the Internet Archive[8], and the FDsys[9] collection jointly operated by the Government

---

[2] The E-Government Act of 2002 (PL 107-347), section 205(a), provides for public access to the opinions of the Federal courts via website. Section 204(c) amends the Judiciary Appropriations Act to read, " the Judicial Conference may, only to the extent necessary, prescribe reasonable fees… to reimburse expenses incurred in providing these services."

[3] As with the fee schedule, a good list of criticisms of PACER's technology is in its entry in Wikipedia (https://en.wikipedia.org/wiki/PACER_(law)), for example Greg Beato's "Tear Down This Paywall" in the June 2012 issue of *Reason* magazine (at http://reason.com/archives/2012/05/30/tear-down-this-paywall), which describes it as "antiquated as a barrister's wig". More recently, the principals of the Free Law Project have published a series of essays on the problems with the system, beginning at https://free.law/2015/03/20/what-is-the-pacer-problem/.

[4] see note iii above.

[5] See, *eg.*, Wolf, Gary, "Who Owns the Law?", WIRED Magazine issue 2.05, May 1994, online at http://archive.wired.com/wired/archive/2.05/the.law.html .

[6] There has never been more robust activity in legal technology than there is at present. The current environment is rich in startup activity; for examples, see documentation on the "Reinvent Law" events held in New York, London, Dubai, and Silicon Valley (many of the talks are available at www.reinventlawchannel.com). At the time of writing, Robert Ambrogi's list legal tech startups numbered 614. It is particularly detailed and helpful. See www.lawsitesblog.com/legal-tech-startups .

[7] https://free.law . The site offers millions of opinions from 420 jurisdictions (see https://www.courtlistener.com/coverage/), and is the current home of the RECAP PACER-harvesting project.

[8] The Internet Archive, at https://archive.org, provides archives of digital documents and multimedia materials at

Publication Office and the Administrative Office of the Courts all offer capabilities that exceed those of PACER in significant ways, particularly in the area of full-text search of cases and its integration with available metadata. Similar examples exist among the state courts, notably at the site maintained by Ohio's Reporter of Decisions for that state's Supreme Court[10], and at the opinions archive run by the Illinois Reporter of Decisions[11].

Third, PACER suffers from a split personality. On one hand, it is an electronic filing and case management system that supports the Federal courts, with an audience of lawyers, judges, and court administrative personnel. On the other – and most important to the public – it is a data-publishing system that offers the work of the Federal courts, both documents and metadata, to a very wide range of people, including litigants, researchers, and government bodies outside the judiciary. It is on PACER's data-publishing function that I will focus now.

That split personality is very much on display in a 2015 article[12] written by two senior staffers from the Administrative Office of the US Courts. Each of the authors has been involved with the design and management of the PACER system for more than 38 years. Their article describes the creation of the specifications for the "NextGen" PACER system. All but a very few of the improvements described in the article are aimed at the e-filing and case-management side of PACER. The innovations intended for the public were largely confined to streamlining the process by which they might file for bankruptcy.

What PACER is not

Equally, there are a number of things that PACER is not.

It is not transparent in its business model or operations. In preparing this testimony, I was repeatedly struck by the difficulty of acquiring information about the design and operation of the system, and about details of the business model on which it is based. I was fortunate to be able to draw on the work of academics and others who have devoted considerable time to puzzling out the little that is known to outsiders.[13] We should all be grateful for their work.

PACER is not an adequate facility for research on the activities of the Federal courts. Social scientists, legal scholars, linguists, and administrators who want to increase the efficiency of court activities – indeed, researchers in a great many disciplines – do not have useful access to PACER's data. That is chiefly because it does not provide bulk access to that data. Significantly, research activities that might be carried out on behalf of the Congress itself are equally impeded. Social Security cases, prisoner

---

staggering scale. A look at https://archive.org/search.php?query=judicial+opinions reveals that the collection is rich in judicial documents and commentary, including but by no means limited to an archive of the RECAP project.

[9] FDsys has its main page at https://www.gpo.gov/fdsys/

[10] The State of Ohio Supreme Court site is at http://www.supremecourt.ohio.gov/.

[11] The Illinois opinions archive is at http://www.illinoiscourts.gov/Opinions/archive.asp.

[12] Brinkema, John, and J. Michael Greenwood. *E-Filing Case Management Services in the US Federal Courts: The Next Generation: A Case Study.* International Journal for Court Administration, vol. 7, n. 1, July 2015. URN:NBN:NL:UI:10-1-115635 . Available online at http://www.iacajournal.org/articles/10.18352/ijca.179/galley/191/download/.

[13] I am especially grateful to Steven Schulze and Carl Malamud, who provided me with comprehensive lists of their earlier work on this subject.

appeals, and immigration matters are all examples of areas in which study of judicial outcomes is important to those who have responsibilities that call for the investigation and evaluation of operations across the full breadth of our system of government. As a practical matter, most of these problems stem ultimately from PACER's failure to provide access to data in bulk.

PACER is not an effective protector of privacy. It contains, and exposes, any amount of personally-identifiable information useful for identity theft[14]. It does not do a good job of protecting the identities of crime victims or of helpful informants (as witness the existence of the website **whosarat.com**[15]). We cannot know the full extent of these problems because, without bulk data access, research or assessment across the full scope of the database is practically impossible.

PACER is not an adequate vehicle for citable legal research. In particular, it does not provide vendor- and medium-neutral identifiers that could provide a basis for either permanent or interim citation, and it retains pagination as the basis for pinpoint citation[16]. Indeed, any identifier that conformed to a uniform scheme for uniquely identifying the opinions of the Federal courts would provide the basis for connection with more traditional citation schemes, but that is lacking.

These are stubborn problems. The sheer size and scope of the document database, the diversity and lack of uniform editorial and classification standards among the courts that originate the documents, and the sensitivity of some of the information all present daunting challenges, some of which have been capably dealt with.

The remaining challenges are not insuperable, provided that the Congress acts. Both the Congress and the Federal courts have strongly and repeatedly announced their commitment to providing full access, even to unpublished opinions, at minimal or no cost. The sentiments expressed by the Congress in the E-Government Act of 2002[17] are echoed in the statements of Justice Alito's committee report supporting Rule 32.1 of the Federal Rules of Administrative Procedure. That Committee pointed out that the E-Government Act of 2002[18] mandated the federal courts (trial courts as well as appellate) to place all their opinions on public Web sites in a text-searchable format – "regardless of whether such opinions are to be published in the official court reporter."[19] Wrote the committee: "The disparity

---

[14] In 2011, Timothy Lee reported research on redaction failures at https://freedom-to-tinker.com/2011/05/25/studying-frequency-redaction-failures-pacer/ . Carl Malamud has done similar work with the detection of Social Security numbers in a small slice of the opinions available in PACER. Interestingly, James Grimmelmann has pointed out that the removal of paywalls from PACER would, to the degree that economic barriers provide practical obscurity, worsen the privacy problem. See https://arstechnica.com/tech-policy/2009/04/case-against-pacer .

[15] https://www.whosarat.com . Founded by an embittered former DEA informant, the site purports to provide information about "informants and agents", information that it at one time acquired by mining PACER for data on individuals who had plea-bargained in multiple Federal criminal cases.

[16] See generally Martin, Peter W., "One District Court's Lonely Gesture Toward Open Access and Medium-Neutral Citation", in his "Citing Legally" blog at http://citeblog.access-to-law.com/?p=797 .

[17] See note ii, above.

[18] See note ii, above.

[19] Memorandum from Hon. Samuel A. Alito to Hon. David F. Levy, at 4 (May 6, 2005), available at http://www.uscourts.gov/rules/Reports/AP5-2005.pdf . Quoted in Martin, Peter. *Finding and Citing the 'Unimportant' Decisions of the United States Courts of Appeal* (2008), online at https://papers.ssrn.com/sol3/papers.cfm?abstract_id=1125484 .

between litigants who are wealthy and those who are not is an unfortunate reality. Undoubtedly, some litigants have better access to unpublished opinions, just as some litigants have better access to published opinions, statutes, law review articles – or, for that matter, lawyers."[20] But the report continued: "[T]he solution is found in measures such as the E-Government Act, which makes unpublished opinions widely available at little or no cost."[21]

What should be done

1. *Fees need to be removed as quickly as possible.* Dissemination fees have strongly inhibited beneficial uses of the data contained in the primary record of the workings of our Federal courts. Consideration should be given to removing per-page viewing fees, or at the very least paring them back to a level that more closely matches PACER's cost of operation. A fee schedule that generates a surplus clearly disregards the will of the Congress as it was stated in the E-Government Act of 2002[22], and subsequently relied upon by Justice Alito's Committee on Appellate Rules in 2005[23]. If instantaneous removal is too disruptive to the processes of judicial administration, a brief sunset period might be considered.

2. *The details of PACER's operations and business model need to be far more visible to the Congress and to the public.* It is nearly impossible for Congress to assess the problem, or for outsiders to make responsible recommendations, given the lack of transparency around PACER. It is far too difficult to find out – for example -- what percentage of PACER's revenue comes from filing fees, how much is derived from data sales to for-profit entities, what expenses are incurred by maintenance and improvements and so on and on. A CRS report describing the business and technical operation of the system in detail would be more than helpful, and would bring welcome clarity to many of the issues involved. To give two examples, outsiders have suggested that the total cost of operation of the system might be recouped exclusively from filing fees, if there were a modest increase; it is also possible that a licensing system that required commercial users of legal information to pay reasonable fees for the raw materials on which their products and businesses are built might do equally well. But without detailed information it is impossible to know for certain, or even to make responsible suggestions.

3. *The users of PACER's data-publication services need representation in the planning and design processes.* The previously-mentioned article on NextGen design[24] shows that input into system design has come exclusively from within the judiciary and from a few "power users" of the e-filing and case-management systems. The designers even chose to ignore the recommendations of their own hired experts – consultants from from MITRE Corporation, a well-respected consulting group that has successfully applied technology to many aspects of judicial administration. There appears to have been little or no consultation with those outside the judiciary who use the publication system, or with outside experts in online dissemination of legal information.

4. *PACER'S data-publishing activities should move to a new home.* The article about PACER's

---

[20] *Id.*, at 6.

[21] *Id.*

[22] See note ii, above.

[23] See note xix, above.

[24] Brinkema and Greenwood, note xii above, p.4

NextGen design, written by two very senior PACER staff members, celebrates the responsiveness of the NextGen design to the needs of the judiciary and to a small group of users of the filing and case-management systems[25]. That can be charitably interpreted as a sound effort to respond to the range of important customers who were in a position to express their needs to the designers. Understandably, those to whom the designers are most immediately responsible are preoccupied with the e-filing and case-management portions of the system -- indeed, the Federal judiciary has from the earliest times preferred to let others take on the chore of publishing their opinions.

Why not, then, put responsibility for data-publishing activities with an organization that has publishing as its primary mission, and the experience and expertise to successfully engage the challenges that the data-publishing side of PACER presents? The Government Publishing Office already has a pilot program for the publication of judicial opinions underway[26]. It is a joint undertaking with the Administrative Office of the Courts. In many ways, it has been highly successful and appears to be scalable to the dimensions that PACER would require. Obviously, the technical problems of transfer from the PACER system have been worked out to a degree, with success that can be built on.

Some assembly will be required. The FDsys collection is based on sound technical underpinnings and data models, but it would need significant expansion. At the moment it covers a relatively small number of courts, and does not extend to the full chronological range available from many of them[27]. The metadata associated with each document is, by comparison with PACER, woefully incomplete (for example, it does not currently contain dates of decision or the names of opinion authors)[28]. Metadata associated with documents in FDsys would need to be brought up, immediately, to the level of embedded metadata available from commercial systems. Removal of the paywall would increase the need for attention to long-neglected privacy concerns.

Ultimately, for the sake of policy, practicality, and fairness, those outside the judiciary should have the same tools available to them as those within it. And ultimately all public data in PACER should be published in formats that encourage its use, using apparatus that facilitates use in bulk[29].

Conclusion

The benefits of bringing PACER back into line with its Congressional mandate, increasing the transparency of its operations, and of placing its publication activities in the hands of those better

---

[25] Brinkema and Greenwood, note xii above, p.5.

[26] The FDsys USCOURTS collection is very briefly described here:
https://www.gpo.gov/help/index.html#about_united_states_courts_opinions.htm

[27] The collection currently contains opinions from 110 courts, representing 885,000 opinions. The collections date back to approximately 2004; there is no set schedule for complete coverage. Private communication from Lisa LaPlant, FDsys program manager, February 7, 2017.

[28] A list of the metadata fields and values available from the FDsys USCOURTS collection is at
https://www.gpo.gov/help/index.html#about_united_states_courts_opinions.htm .

[29] The Free Law Project provides bulk data services via their web site at https://free.law . Examples of bulk metadata services for government information abound; the best ones at present are outside the United States, although courts everywhere have been slow to provide access to their metadata in bulk. For example, see the UK Data.gov.uk project at https://data.gov.uk/ .

equipped to carry them out, are many. First and foremost will be the removal of barriers that prevent the public from reading the opinions of the courts for themselves, and from exercising the right to know the laws that govern them. Publication systems that permit research utilizing the full range of data available from PACER will make it easier for the Congress to fulfill its responsibilities, improve the efficiency and functioning of the judiciary, and stimulate new approaches to legal information and encourage new and innovative businesses.

Thank you for the opportunity to testify today. I look forward to your questions.

Mr. Issa. Thank you.
Professor Geyh.

TESTIMONY OF CHARLES G. GEYH, JOHN F. KIMERLING PROFESSOR OF LAW, INDIANA LAW SCHOOL

Mr. Geyh. Mr. Chairman, it is a privilege to serve—to appear before the Subcommittee I served on.

Mr. Issa. Perhaps the microphone a little closer in and on.

Mr. Geyh. There we go. If I turn it on, it works better.

Mr. Issa. Superb.

Mr. Geyh. It is a privilege to appear before the Subcommittee that I served as counsel nearly 25 years ago, dry gulp.

The Constitution works and the judiciary it established works because we believe it works. If we lose that faith in the judicial system, Congress can gut its budget, the President can defy its orders, and the role the Framers envisioned for the judiciary keeping the other branches in check will be lost. And so I do share Mr. Nadler and Mr. Conyers' concern that there is a difference between robust criticism, which I think we need, it is essential to accountability; and assaults on the legitimacy of the judiciary as an institution, which do worry me because the judiciary is fragile in that regard. Unlike Congress, which derives their legitimacy from the voters, the judiciary doesn't have voters. They derive their legitimacy from their perceived integrity, their perceived impartiality, their perceived independence, which really is the subject of this hearing today, because the mechanisms, like recusal, like discipline, like codes of conduct, like disclosure are ways that we hold the judiciary accountable. They are the ways that we hold the judiciary, you know, make sure that the judiciary is legitimate.

To those ends, let me talk first briefly about disqualification. I think the substantive standards are fine. I think that there is a concern, though, with process. Congress has not legislated the process for disqualification, which means that it is all over the map. And the norm that worries me most is the norm that judges get to decide their own disqualification, which is like grading your own homework.

I think it is problematic, from an appearance standpoint, for judges to be put in a position of being asked, are you too impartial to sit, too partial to sit, and the person who answers that is the judge who may be too partial to sit. I mean, we need to work on that one.

Second, when it comes to codes of conduct, the Judicial Conference promulgated codes beginning in 1973, and they are terrific. Unfortunately, the Supreme Court does not have a code that applies to it, and I think that is a problem. Twenty-five thousand judges in the United States, nine are not subject to a code of ethics and they are the most powerful judges in the country. The optics are bad.

Now, the Chief Justice tells us that they don't need a code because they consult the code that applies to the lower Federal courts. The trouble with that is that you know and I know that you are going to react differently to a code that applies to someone else as opposed to a body of rules that applies to you, and the exhibit A for that would be Justice Ginsburg from last fall when she starts criticizing then candidate Donald Trump, under circumstances in which the Code of Conduct says, no, you don't. Two days later, she retracts those statements after the code is called to her attention. I would like to think that if they had a code and bound themselves to it, this problem would never have occurred.

Turning to discipline. The disciplinary process has been in place since Congress created it in 1980. It did fall into some disrepair about 10 years ago, and thanks to the vigilance of this Committee, the process got jump-started. And I would like to congratulate the Judicial Conference for making some significant improvements in 2008 and again in 2015 that have made it work better.

My lingering concern, frankly, is that—with the disciplinary process is that, the statutory standard is exceedingly vague. Misconduct is defined with reference to conduct that is prejudicial to the effective and expeditious administration of the business of the courts. I worry a little bit that that lets the judiciary do whatever they want to and—or more—and that is too strong. I think they do a conscientious job. But the trouble is that from a perception standpoint, that can mean just about anything.

The solution that virtually every State has employed is to say we can have this general disciplinary standard, but we define it with reference to the Code of Conduct. Has the judge violated the Code of Conduct? If so, then is the violation severe enough to warrant discipline? But by tethering this very vague standard to the code, everybody understands what the operative rules are and when a judge is going to be at risk.

Finally, I didn't talk about this at length in my testimony, in my written testimony, but a point about disclosure. You know, I think that the financial disclosure statements are essential for the general public, they are essential for—they are essential for lawyers who have clients who appear before judges, and they are essential for watchdog organizations. My concern is that we still don't have a system in place where we are enabling the public to get ready and open access online to those disclosure statements.

I understand where the judiciary is concerned, and I suspect the judiciary's primary concern is for the safety and security of its judges. There are nasty people out there who appear before judges, and they worry that information about the judge's family and addresses can be problematic. That, I think, is best resolved by redaction rules and not by hiding the ball when it comes to forms that the public is legitimately entitled to receive. Thank you.

[The prepared statement of Mr. Geyh follows:]

TESTIMONY OF CHARLES G. GEYH
"JUDICIAL TRANSPARENCY AND ETHICS"
HEARING BEFORE THE HOUSE COMMITTEE ON THE JUDICIARY'S
SUBCOMMITTEE ON COURTS, INTELLECTUAL PROPERTY, AND THE
INTERNET

FEBRUARY 14, 2017

My name is Charles G. Geyh (pronounced "Jay"). I am the John F. Kimberling Professor of Law at the Indiana University Maurer School of Law, in Bloomington Indiana. My writings on judicial conduct, ethics, selection, independence, accountability, and administration include more than seventy books, book chapters, articles, reports, and other publications. I am a coauthor of the treatise *Judicial Conduct and Ethics* (Lexis Law Publishing, 5th ed. 2013), and author of *Courting Peril: The Political Transformation of the American Judiciary* (Oxford University Press 2016); *Judicial Disqualification: An Analysis of Federal Law* (Federal Judicial Center 2010); and *When Courts & Congress Collide: The Struggle for Control of America's Judicial System* (University of Michigan Press 2006). In addition, I have served as co-Reporter to the ABA Joint Commission to Revise the Model Code of Judicial Conduct. Prior to entering academia in 1991, I was counsel to the House Judiciary Committee's Subcommittee on Courts, Intellectual Property and the Administration of Justice, under Chairman Robert W. Kastenmeier.

INTRODUCTION

Our Constitution works only because we believe it works. We believe in the tripartite system of government that our founders framed. We believe in the checks and balances that system provides, and in the role that a strong, separate and independent judiciary plays in keeping the executive and legislative branches in check. As a consequence, we accept the judgments of our courts even if we do not agree with them.

If we lose faith in the judiciary, the system of government that has served us well for over two and quarter centuries falls like a house of cards. The judiciary cannot fund itself. It is dependent on Congress for that. Courts cannot enforce their own orders. They are dependent on the President for that. If we lose trust and confidence in the judiciary, court budgets can easily be gutted, court rulings defied, and the constitutional order—which depends on courts keeping Congress and the President in check via judicial review—will collapse.

In other words, the survival of our courts depends on their perceived legitimacy with the people they serve. The reason that President Trump's recent reference to District Judge James Robart as a "so-called judge" raised concern, is because it transcended robust criticism of a judicial decision and challenged the legitimacy of the court itself. I share conservative scholar William Baude's characterization of this development as "deadly serious," because it reveals the judiciary's vulnerability to defiance, and the fragility of the constitutional order if court rulings are not respected as legitimate.

The Robart episode underscores the vital role that this subcommittee plays in protecting and promoting the legitimacy of the courts—legitimacy upon which the nation depends. Unlike Congress and the President, federal judges are appointed. As a consequence, federal judges do not derive their legitimacy from the electorate. Rather, federal judges derive legitimacy from the respect they command as a result of their perceived competence, impartiality, independence, and integrity. Judicial competence, impartiality, independence, and integrity, in turn, are promoted by three mechanisms of relevance to this hearing: disqualification, codes of judicial conduct, and disciplinary processes. I will discuss each of these in order.

DISQUALIFICATION REFORM

For centuries, impartiality has been a defining feature of the Anglo-American judge's role in the administration of justice. The reason is clear: in a constitutional order grounded in the rule of law, it is imperative that judges make decisions according to law, unclouded by personal bias or conflicts of interest. When the impartiality of a judge is in doubt, the appropriate remedy is to disqualify that judge from hearing further proceedings in the matter.

Disqualification has ethical and procedural dimensions. The ethical dimension is governed by Canon 3C of the Code of Conduct for United States Judges, as construed by the Codes of Conduct Committee of the Judicial Conference of the United States. The procedural dimension is governed primarily by sections 455 and 144 in Title 28 of the United States Code. The text of Canon 3C is substantially similar to 28 U.S.C. § 455; yet while both seek to promote public confidence in the judiciary, each maintains a separate focus. The Code of Conduct endeavors to inform federal judges of their ethical obligations to the end of advising them on how judges should conduct themselves. Section 455, however, is a procedural statute aimed at articulating disqualification standards to the end of preserving the rights of litigants to impartial justice.

My focus here is on sections 455 and 144 of Title 28. In my view, section 455 does an effective job of articulating substantive disqualification standards, which are largely uniform across federal and state court systems. I do, however, have some concerns with disqualification procedure, and recommend that the Committee consider legislation to address the problem inherent in having a judge who is accused of bias or conflict of interest be the judge who decides whether that accusation has merit. As it stands, section 144, in contrast, is a virtual dead letter, and should either be eliminated or amended to serve its original purpose.

28 U.S.C. § 455 and Judicial Self-Disqualification

In the federal system, the norm is that disqualification motions are decided by the judge whose disqualification is sought.[1] While it may be a bit awkward to initiate the disqualification process by calling upon the party who seeks a judge's disqualification to raise the matter with that judge, it is a defensible approach. The target judge will be the most familiar with the facts giving rise to the motion, and can step aside without delay when circumstances warrant.

When, however, the judge is disinclined to step aside, asking that judge to resolve a contested disqualification motion becomes much more problematic. In effect, such an approach calls upon the judge to "grade his own paper"—to ask the judge who is accused of being too biased to decide the case, to decide whether he is too biased to decide the case. Unsurprisingly, two commentators observe that "the fact that judges in many jurisdictions decide on their own disqualification and recusal challenges . . . is one of the most heavily criticized features of U.S. disqualification law, and for good reason."[2] Another commentator adds:

> The appearance of partiality and the perils of self-serving statutory interpretation suggest that, to the extent logistically feasible, another judge should preside over [disqualification] motions. To permit the judge whose conduct or relationships prompted the motion to decide the motion erodes the necessary public confidence in the integrity of a judicial system, which should rely on the presence of a neutral and detached judge to preside over all court proceedings.[3]

And yet another commentator echoes that "[t]he Catch-22 of the law of disqualification is that the very judge being challenged for bias or interest is almost always the one who, at least in the first instance, decides whether she is too conflicted to sit on the case."[4]

Over eighty percent of the public thinks that disqualification motions should be decided by a different judge.[5] The assumption underlying the public's view—that a judge is ill-positioned to assess the extent of her own bias (real or perceived)—is corroborated

---

[1] Schurz Communications, Inc. v. FCC, 982 F.2d 1057, 1059 (7th Cir. 1992); *In re* United States, 158 F.3d 26, 34 (1st Cir. 1998) (citations omitted). *Accord* United States v. Heldt, 668 F.2d 1238, 1271 (D.C. Cir. 1981).

[2] James Sample, David Pozen, *Making Judicial Recusal More Rigorous*, 46 JUDGES' J. 17, 21 (2007).

[3] Leslie W. Abrahamson, *Deciding Recusal Motions: Who Judges the Judges?*, 28 VAL. U. L. REV. 543, 561 (1994).

[4] Amanda Frost, *Keeping Up Appearances: A Process Oriented Approach to Judicial Recusal*, 53 U. KAN. L. REV. 531, 571 (2005).

[5] Press Release, Justice at Stake Campaign, Poll: Huge Majority Wants Firewall Between Judges, Election Backers (Feb. 22, 2009) (on file with author). Is this on file with you?

by empirical research. Recent empirical studies in cognitive psychology have demonstrated that judges, like lay people, are susceptible to cognitive biases in their decision-making.[6] But they have trouble spotting those biases. People typically rely on introspection to assess their own biases;[7] however, "because many biases work below the surface and leave no trace of their operation, an introspective search for evidence of bias often turns up empty."[8] The individual thus takes his unfruitful search as proof that bias is not present and fails to correct for those biases.[9]

The peril of asking a person to assess the extent of her own bias is further exacerbated for judges, who are being asked to assess whether they harbor a real or perceived biases that their oaths of office and codes of conduct direct them to avoid. Conceding real or perceived bias in such circumstances can thus be misconstrued as failing their duty of impartiality, which helps to explain why some take umbrage at disqualification requests. In short, the tradition of calling upon judges to be the final arbiters of challenges to their own impartiality should be abandoned.

A simple solution to the problem of calling upon a judge to evaluate her own qualification to sit is to assign the matter to a different judge. Such a procedure could be limited to courts of original jurisdiction (district judges, magistrates, bankruptcy judges), or extended to appellate courts. Illinois employs such a procedure with language that could be borrowed, with appropriate modifications to accommodate the vocabulary of section 455: "Upon the filing of a petition for substitution of judge for cause, a hearing to determine whether the cause exists shall be conducted as soon as possible by a judge other than the judge named in the petition."[10] The Illinois statute adds that the judge whose disqualification is sought "need not testify but may submit an affidavit if the judge wishes" to assist the judge evaluating the disqualification petition.[11]

28 U.S.C. § 144 Reform

Section 144 of Title 28 states in its entirety:

> Whenever a party to any proceeding in a district court makes and files a timely and sufficient affidavit that the judge before whom the matter is pending has a personal bias or prejudice either against him or in favor of any adverse party, such judge shall proceed no further therein, but another judge shall be assigned to hear such proceeding.
> The affidavit shall state the facts and the reasons for the belief that bias or prejudice exists, and shall be filed not less than ten days before the beginning of the term at which the proceeding is to be heard, or good cause shall be shown for failure to file it within such time. A party may file only one such affidavit in

---

[6] Daniel Kahneman & Shane Frederick, *Representativeness Revisited: Attribute Substitution in Intuitive Judgment*, in Heuristics and Biases: The Psychology of Intuitive Judgment 49, 49-50 (Thomas Gilovich et al., eds., 2002); Guthric et al., *Inside the Judicial Mind*, 86 Cornell L. Rev. 777 (2001).

[7] Emily Pronin et al., *Valuing Thoughts, Ignoring Behavior: The Introspection Illusion as a Source of the Bias Blind Spot*, 43 J. OF EXPERIMENTAL SOC. PSYCHOL. 565, 565-67 (2007).

[8] Ehrlinger, *supra* note 8, at 10.

[9] Pronin, *supra* note 9, at 565–67.

[10] 735 Ill. Comp. Stat. 5/2-1001 (a)(3).

[11] *Id.*

any case. It shall be accompanied by a certificate of counsel of record stating that it is made in good faith.[12]

A literal reading of section 144 suggests that a party can force disqualification automatically, simply by filing an affidavit alleging that the judge is biased against the affiant or in favor of the affiant's opponent. Such an interpretation would render section 144 akin to peremptory disqualification procedures adopted by judicial systems in a number of western states—and the legislative history of section 144 lends some support for this interpretation of the section.[13]

The federal courts have indeed held that under section 144 a judge must step aside upon the filing of a facially sufficient affidavit, but they have been exacting in their interpretations, not only of what a facially sufficient affidavit requires, but of the procedural prerequisites to application of the statute as well. Thus, motions have been dismissed because the motion was untimely, because the movant failed to submit an affidavit, because the movant submitted more than one affidavit, because the attorney rather than a party submitted the affidavit, because the movant's affidavit was unaccompanied by a certificate of counsel, because the affidavit failed to make allegations with particularity, and because the certificate of counsel certified only to the affiant's good faith, not counsel's.[14]

This is not accidental. As the First Circuit explained, "courts have responded to the draconian procedure—automatic transfer based solely on one side's affidavit—by insisting on a firm showing in the affidavit that the judge does have a personal bias or prejudice to a party."[15] In a similar vein, the Seventh Circuit has stated:

> [T]he facts averred must be sufficiently definite and particular to convince a reasonable person that bias exists; simple conclusions, opinions, or rumors are insufficient. . . . Because the statute 'is heavily weighed in favor of recusal,' its requirements are to be strictly construed to prevent abuse.[16]

As a consequence, section 144 has been rendered a much more cumbersome tool to obtain disqualification than section 455, even though the latter calls upon judges to evaluate the merits of a movant's allegations and not simply the facial sufficiency of

---

[12] 28 U.S.C. § 144 (1949). Originally enacted as § 21 of the Judicial Code of 1911, the statute was recodified as § 144 in 1948 without significant change.

[13] 46 Cong. Rec. 2627 (1911) (remarks of Representative Cullop).

[14] *See, e.g.*, United States v. Barnes, 909 F.2d 1059, 1072 (7th Cir. 1990) (counsel did not present certificate of good faith, "another requirement of section 144 with which Barnes failed to comply"); *In re* Cooper & Lynn, 821 F.2d 833, 838 (1st Cir. 1987) ("[N]o *party* filed an affidavit. . . . Rather the affidavit was filed by an attorney."); United States v. Merkt, 794 F.2d 950, 961 (5th Cir. 1986) ("Elder's affidavit violates the one-affidavit rule . . . and need not be considered."); United States v. Balistrieri, 779 F.2d 1191, 1200 (7th Cir. 1985) ("Because of the statutory limitation that a party may file only one affidavit in a case, we need consider only the affidavit filed with Balistrieri's first motion."); Roberts v. Bailar, 625 F.2d 125, 128 (6th Cir. 1980) (motion rejected because counsel, not plaintiff, signed and filed affidavit); United States *ex rel.* Wilson v. Coughlin, 472 F.2d 100, 104 (7th Cir. 1973) (same); Morrison v. United States, 432 F.2d 1227, 1229 (5th Cir. 1970) (motion rejected because there was no certificate of good faith by counsel); United States v. Hoffa, 382 F.2d 856, 860 (6th Cir. 1967) (same).

[15] *In re* Martinez-Catala, 129 F.3d 213, 218 (1st Cir. 1997).

[16] United States v. Sykes, 7 F.3d 1331, 1339 (7th Cir. 1993) (citation omitted).

those allegations. Judges who are loath to tolerate strategic manipulation of disqualification rules have imposed what many commentators have long regarded as an unduly stingy construction of section 144.[17] An additional reason that section 144 has fallen into relative disuse is that it requires the more difficult showing of actual bias, whereas section 455(a) requires a mere appearance of bias. Section 455 thus subsumes section 144. As the Supreme Court has observed of section 144, it "seems to be properly invocable only when section 55(a) can be invoked anyway."[18] Moreover, many of the circumstances that might qualify as actual bias under section 144 are specifically enumerated in section 455(b), which explicitly addresses various conflicts of interest, in addition to actual bias.[19] In short, while parties still file motions under section 144, they usually do so in tandem with section 455, with the latter section typically monopolizing the court's attention.

Section 144 has been rendered a problematic and cumbersome tool for disqualification, leaving section 455 as the one workable mechanism for disqualification in the federal system. One simple solution is to decommission section 144 after nearly a century of service. A second possibility, however, is to return to the roots of section 144 and explore alternative means to achieve its objective. That objective was to provide a party with a relatively simple means to request a different judge without putting the original judge in a position to second guess the merits of the party's request. The pitfall of section 144 was its requirement that the moving party submit a "timely and sufficient affidavit" charging the judge with personal bias. By hinging disqualification on a facially sufficient allegation of bias, the underlying truth of which could not be challenged, the statute simultaneously encouraged litigants to exaggerate their assertions of bias to meet the threshold of facial sufficiency, and angered judges targeted with exaggerated claims, who responded by making the threshold requirements more exacting.

The problems of section 144 could be avoided if the statute were amended to offer parties a limited opportunity to request a simple substitution of judges, much in the nature of the preemptory challenge in jury selection. Nineteen states currently employ a procedure of this kind. Typically it is limited to trial judges. It may only be invoked one time by each party. And it must be invoked early in the proceedings.

The primary objection to substitution procedures is that a party may use them strategically to avoid judges who, while impartial, are likely to be unsympathetic to the party's claims on the merits. The short answer to this concern is that a party is entitled only to one substitution per case, which limits the harm—a harm more than offset by the benefit of avoiding the aggravation and expenditure of resources associated with litigating traditional disqualification claims. A secondary objection relates to the administrative burdens associated with implementing judicial substitution procedures. While this is a legitimate concern, it has not proved insurmountable in the nearly twenty jurisdictions that employ them (including rural jurisdictions like Alaska and Montana).

CODES OF JUDICIAL CONDUCT AND THE U.S. SUPREME COURT

---

[17] John Frank, *Disqualification of Judges*, 56 YALE L.J. 605, 629 (1947).

[18] Liteky v. United States, 510 U.S. 540, 548 (1994).

[19] *See id.* ("[S]ection 455 is the more modern and complete recusal statute.").

In 1922 the American Bar Association established a Committee, then chaired by Chief Justice William Howard Taft, which promulgated Canons of Judicial Ethics that the ABA adopted in 1924[20]—a series of thirty-four hortatory pronouncements "intended to be nothing more than the American Bar Association's suggestions for guidance of individual judges."[21] In 1972, the ABA approved a "Model Code of Judicial Conduct," comprised of seven broadly worded canons and a series of more specific provisions underlying each canon, specifying a judge's ethical obligations in greater detail. The ABA substantially revised the Model Code in 1990 and again in 2007. Today, all fifty state judicial systems have promulgated codes of conduct applicable to their judges, based on one of the three ABA models.

For its part, the Judicial Conference of the United States adopted its Code of Conduct for U.S. Judges in 1973, based on the 1972 Model Code, and has modified its code several times in the years since. In addition, the Judicial Conference has authorized its Committee on Codes of Conduct to issue Ethics Advisory Opinions, 115 of which are available online.[22] The Committee on Codes of Conduct, also known as the "Dear Abby Committee," also offers confidential advice to judges upon request, in response to ethical questions they raise.

In my view, the Judicial Conference has done a good job of maintaining and explicating its Code. Three members of the federal judiciary participated actively in the 2007 ABA Model Code revision project, which underscores how seriously the federal judiciary takes the project. And the Committee on Code of Conduct's ongoing efforts underscore that the Judicial Conference regards the Code as more than window-dressing—the Code is being revised and referenced on an ongoing basis.

Although the Judicial Conference is led by the Chief Justice of the United States, its jurisdiction is limited to the lower federal courts. Thus, the Code of Conduct for U.S. Judges applies to all federal judges except justices on the Supreme Court of the United States.[23] And therein lies the problem. I would encourage this subcommittee to consider legislation that calls upon the Supreme Court to promulgate a Code of Conduct applicable to itself.

There are 25,000 judicial officers in the United States, all but nine of whom—the most visible and influential nine in the nation—are subject to a code of judicial conduct. No ethics rule prevents a Supreme Court justice from engaging in political activity, participating in ex parte communications, or joining a club that discriminates based on race, sex, religion, or national origin. Yet ethics rules for all other federal judges forbid these activities.

---

[20] JOHN P. MACKENZIE, THE APPEARANCE OF JUSTICE 181–83 (1974).

[21] Robert Martineau, *Enforcement of the Code of Judicial Conduct*, 1972 UTAH L. REV. 410, 411.

[22] *Guide to Judiciary Policy, Vol. 2B, Ch. 2: Published Advisory Opinions* (2016), http://www.uscourts.gov/sites/default/files/vol02b-ch02.pdf.

[23] For an analysis and discussion of the issue of applying the Code of Conduct for U.S. Judges to the Supreme Court, *see* James J. Alfini, *Supreme Court Ethics: The Need for Greater Transparency and Accountability*, 21 PROF. LAW. 10 (2012).

Codes of ethics for judges fortify the administration of justice. They tell judges their ethical responsibilities and articulate high standards of conduct to which they should aspire. They assure litigants that the judges before whom they appear are committed to fairness and impartiality. They require judges to conduct their personal and professional lives in in a manner that will foster respect for the courts.

In his 2011 year-end report on the federal judiciary, Chief Justice Roberts said that the Supreme Court did not need to adopt a code of conduct because the justices already "consult" the Code of Conduct for United States Judges, which governs other federal judges. [24] I have two concerns. First, it is unrealistic to think that judges will in fact consult a code they have not approved and agreed to follow, as reliably as one they have. Last year, Justice Ruth Bader Ginsburg publicly criticized then presidential candidate Donald Trump, only to express regret for those remarks shortly thereafter, explaining that, "[j]udges should avoid commenting on a candidate for public office." Canon 5(A)(2) of the Code of Conduct provides that a judge should not "publicly endorse or oppose a candidate for public office." Had Justice Ginsburg consulted the Code before, rather than after this episode, perhaps the problem could have been avoided.

Second, there is an obvious difference between consulting a code that a justice remains free to disregard, and binding oneself to a code that a justice is committed to follow. Justices Thomas and Scalia were widely criticized for serving as featured speakers at Federalist Society events, given commentary accompanying Canon 4(C) of the Code of Conduct for U.S. Judges, which states that "[a] judge may attend fund-raising events of law-related and other organizations although the judge may not be a speaker, a guest of honor, or featured on the program of such an event." Insofar as the Code was called to the attention of the justices involved, it was apparently disregarded—which the justices were free to do. There is an argument to make that Supreme Court justices should be permitted to speak at such events: the public's interest in what they have to say may offset the concern that they are lending the prestige of their offices to advance the interests of the organization that sells more tickets by hosting them. Indeed, the latest version of the ABA Model Code of Judicial Conduct allows judges to speak in such circumstances. [25] If the Supreme Court shares the ABA's view and had simply adopted a code that followed the ABA Model on this point, it could have avoided the perception that its justices were behaving unethically.

Skeptics have argued that it would be an empty gesture for the Supreme Court to adopt a code because there is no workable way to enforce compliance. But the pledge itself has value. Just as the public rightly expects judges to follow their oaths of office, it will also assume that a justice who vows to abide by ethics rules that the Court itself adopted will do so.

---

[24] *2011 Year-End Report on the Federal Judiciary*, http://www.supremecourt.gov/publicinfo/year-end/2011year-endreport.pdf.

[25] ABA Model Code of Judicial Conduct, Rule 3.7(A)(4).

The Chief Justice has said that constitutional limits on congressional power to regulate the Supreme Court are largely untested. But the U.S. Constitution delegates to Congress the powers to regulate the Court's appellate jurisdiction and to make laws necessary and proper for "carrying into execution" all powers vested by the Constitution in the government of the United States. Advocates of original intent might note that the founding generation interpreted those powers broadly to permit Congress to regulate the size of the Supreme Court, where, when and how often the Court meets, how many justices constitute a quorum, and the duties of the justices themselves—including a duty to "ride circuit" and hear cases as trial judges. Legislation requiring the Court to write its own code of ethics falls well within this congressional power.

This is not a partisan issue. Judges appointed by presidents of both parties confront ethical dilemmas. Codes of judicial conduct proliferated in the Watergate era amid pervasive suspicion of government that has not dissipated in the ensuing forty years. It would be unfortunate if the only judges in the United States who see no need for a code of ethics were those on the nation's most powerful tribunal.

THE DISCIPLINARY PROCESS AND ITS DISCONNECTION FROM THE CODE OF CONDUCT

In the federal system, circuit judicial councils were established in 1939 to administer the federal courts in each of the regional circuits.[26] The circuit judicial councils exercised limited informal regulatory authority over judicial conduct, until their disciplinary role was formalized in 1980, when Congress enacted the Judicial Councils Reform and Judicial Conduct and Disability Act.[27] That Act authorized judicial councils in each of the thirteen federal circuits to investigate complaints against federal judges and administer discipline for conduct deemed "prejudicial to the effective and expeditious administration of the business of the courts."[28] In 1993, the National Commission on Judicial Discipline and Removal issued a report on the disciplinary system, which concluded that it was working "reasonably well."[29]

As of the turn of the new millennium, however, circumstances had changed. The infrequency of formal judicial self-discipline aroused suspicion among members of the House Judiciary Committee and the general public. Congressman Sensenbrenner introduced legislation to establish an Inspector General within the Judicial Branch[30] to

---

[26] Charles Gardner Geyh, *Informal Methods of Judicial Discipline*, 142 U. PA. L. REV. 243, 261–71 (1993).

[27] Judicial Councils Reform and Judicial Conduct and Disability Act of 1980, Pub. L. No. 96-458, 94 Stat. 2035 (1980).

[28] 28 U.S.C. § 351(a).

[29] Robert W. Kastenmeier, *Report of the National Commission on Judicial Discipline & Removal*, 152 F.R.D. 265, 280, 362, 363 (1994).

[30] Justice for All Act of 2004, Pub. L. No. 108-405 (2004), https://www.congress.gov/108/plaws/publ405/PLAW-108publ405.pdf.

oversee the disciplinary process, and the Committee initiated an impeachment inquiry into the conduct of a district judge whose disciplinary proceedings had languished.[31]

The Chief Justice responded by appointing a Committee headed by Justice Stephen Breyer, which issued a report in 2006.[32] The Breyer Committee Report found fault with the disciplinary process, particularly in high-profile cases, and recommended reforms that the Judicial Conference implemented in 2008. In 2014, the Judicial Conference Committee on Judicial Conduct and Disability proposed additional changes that the Judicial Conference approved in 2015.[33]

I credit this Committee's efforts a decade ago, with jump-starting the disciplinary process that had stalled and fallen into disrepair. Given the Judicial Conference's renewed sense of vigilance, I see no continuing need to add a layer of government in the form of an inspector general.

I do, however, have one lingering concern with the disciplinary process that is better addressed via oversight than legislation. Under the statute, judicial conduct is assessed with reference to whether it is "prejudicial to the effective and expeditious administration of the business of the courts." So general a standard offers no clear guidance as to what does or does not constitute misconduct, and contributes to under-enforcement, insofar as judicial councils are reluctant to impose sanctions on judges for conduct that the judges may not know violates the statute.

There is an easy and obvious solution: the Judicial Conference can tether its interpretation of the statute more tightly to its Code of Conduct. The ABA Model Code of Judicial Conduct expressly states that it is designed for use by judicial conduct organizations in disciplinary proceedings, and its use for that purpose is ubiquitous among state systems. The Judicial Conference, however, has resisted a move in that direction, with the explanation that:

---

[31] *Impeaching Manuel L. Real, a Judge of the United States District Court for the Central District of California, for High Crimes and Misdemeanors: Hearing on H. Res. 916 Before the Subcommittee on Courts, the Internet, and Intellectual Property*, 109th Cong. (2006), https://www.gpo.gov/fdsys/pkg/CHRG-109hhrg29969/pdf/CHRG-109hhrg29969.pdf.

[32] The Judicial Conduct and Disability Act Study Committee, *Implementation of the Judicial Conduct and Disability Act of 1980*, SUPREME COURT.GOV (2006), https://www.supremecourt.gov/publicinfo/breyercommitteereport.pdf.

[33] *Guide to Judiciary Policy, Vol. 2E, Ch. 3: Rules for Judicial-Conduct and Judicial-Disability Proceedings* (2016), http://www.uscourts.gov/sites/default/files/guide-vol02e-ch03.pdf. Professor Arthur Hellman analyzes these amendments in *Proposed Amendments to the Federal Judicial Misconduct Rules: Comments and Suggestions* (U. of Pittsburgh Leg. Stud. Research Paper No. 2015-10, 2015), https://papers.ssrn.com/sol3/papers.cfm?abstract_id=2554596. Professor Hellman, who has appeared before this subcommittee numerous times over the years, and with whom the subcommittee would be well advised to consult moving forward, has recommended a number of legislative reforms worth the subcommittee's consideration. *See* Arthur D. Hellman, *The Federal Judicial Conduct and Disability System: Unfinished Business for Congress and for the Judiciary* (U. of Pittsburgh Legal Studies Research Paper No. 2014-19, 2013), https://papers.ssrn.com/sol3/papers.cfm?abstract_id=2435287.

> Although the Code of Conduct for United States Judges may be informative, its main precepts are highly general; the Code is in many potential applications aspirational rather than a set of disciplinary rules. Ultimately, the responsibility for determining what constitutes misconduct under the statute is the province of the judicial council of the circuit, subject to such review and limitations as are ordained by the statute and by these Rules.[34]

Such an assessment is patently incorrect: As just noted, state judiciaries across the country routinely rely on code of conduct violations as a basis for discipline. However "highly general" the Code of Conduct may be (and I do not think it is much of the time), it is much less general than the statutory language.

That said, I fully understand where minor or inadvertent Code violations may not give rise to misconduct sufficient to meet the statutory standard and warrant discipline. But I have *never* come upon a case of judicial misconduct warranting discipline that did not violate the Code of Judicial Conduct. Hence, the appropriate approach is to begin with the Code of Judicial Conduct, to determine if it was violated, and if so, whether the violation was egregious enough to meet the statutory standard. Such an approach gives the Code of Judicial Conduct added muscle and reassures the public that the decision to discipline a judge or not is guided by a code, and not just the unguided discretion of the judge's brethren in the judge's circuit.

CONCLUSION

The survival of our courts depends on their perceived legitimacy with the people they serve. Federal judges derive legitimacy from the respect they command as a result of their competence, impartiality, independence, and integrity. Those values are promoted through an ethics infrastructure that includes disqualification procedures, codes of judicial conduct, and disciplinary processes. In my view, that infrastructure is sound. The federal judiciary deserves our respect as a corps of honorable and dedicated women and men who are committed to upholding the rule of law. That is not to suggest that there are no problems. There are—and I have made several recommendations. First, I recommend that 28 U.S.C. § 455 be amended to limit the practice of judges "grading their own homework," by ruling on their own disqualification. Second, I recommend that 28 U.S.C. § 144 be removed or amended to serve its original purpose as a limited mechanism to permit one-time substitution of judges. Third, I recommend legislation that calls upon the Supreme Court of the United States to join every other court in the nation and adopt a code of conduct. Fourth, I recommend that this committee work with the Judicial Conference to clarify its disciplinary standards by tethering them more tightly to the Code of Conduct for U.S. Judges.

---

[34] Guide to Judicial Policy, Ch. 3: Rules for Judicial Conduct and Judicial Disability Proceedings 7 (2016), http://www.uscourts.gov/sites/default/files/guide-vol02c-ch03.pdf.

Mr. ISSA. I thank all three of you. I will now recognize myself for a round of questioning.

And I would like to ask unanimous consent that the statement by Professor Jonathan Zittrain be placed in the record in which, es-sentially, he offers to make available PACER for free.* And I will begin there.

Mr. ISSA. Professor Bruce, is that viable? Is it viable to simply offload all of the information of the courts, potentially, to make it free without commercial advertising?

Mr. BRUCE. It is very difficult to tell, and that is part of the rea-son that I am interested in getting more detailed reporting of PAC-ER's finances, and people have made various suggestions over the years. There is some thought that, for example, the entire cost of covering PACER could be generated through filing fees. There is also—there is also the possibility that one could go into some form of commercial licensing for those who are actually making commer-cial use of the data as another possible source of revenue.

But all of those, at this point, are merely informed guesses be-cause the finances of PACER are not particularly transparent. I re-ceived this morning, as you have, a bunch of information about PACER's financials that I have not seen before.

As far as operating from a third party point of view, if someone were to hand that to us tomorrow, it would be difficult to do.

I do think that the people who are operating FDsys at the Gov-ernment Publishing Office are in a good position to do it. They are a quarter of the way there already in terms of the number of courts that they are covering.

Mr. ISSA. Thank you.

Now we go to cameras in the courtroom. Mr. Osterreicher, let me move away from cameras in the courtroom directly and just go a round of quick questioning for my own edification. Is it reasonable to assume that since the courts in most areas of the country allow witnesses to be video deposed and those depositions, in video form, are admissible, that in fact video has a practical value to juries making decisions?

Mr. OSTERREICHER. I think it absolutely does. Part of a jury's function is to look at the demeanor, character of those people testi-fying. Sometimes just seeing a transcript or even just hearing the audio is not enough. So I think that video is a very important com-ponent.

I also think, even though most court proceedings are not very compelling television, if you have high quality——

Mr. ISSA. But you have been there for the good ones.

Mr. OSTERREICHER. Yes. But even then, sometimes, you know, it has been said that most courtroom proceedings are like watching paint dry. It just is not the Perry Mason confession moments that we are used to seeing in an hour's worth of television.

But that said, I think they are far more interesting than just the transcripts and audio themselves. Though, in the alternative, as we have seen just recently, there are a lot of people that wanted to hear that oral argument in the Ninth Circuit.

---

*Note: The material referred to is not printed in this hearing record but is on file with the Subcommittee, and can also be accessed at:

http://docs.house.gov/Committee/Calendar/ByEvent.aspx?EventID=105547

Mr. ISSA. That is one thing we can count on is, even when paint's drying, somebody will dump the bucket every once in awhile and it will get very exciting in the room.

Professor Geyh, I want to spend the rest of my time asking a few questions on ethics. You mentioned conflicts of interest, and this is a great question. Do you believe that we have the obligation to ensure that a system is in place that is verifiable as to people who have conflicts and thus there has to be disclosure in order to determine whether there may be a hidden conflict?

Mr. GEYH. I would agree.

Mr. ISSA. Do you believe that, at a minimum, a body in camera must make that decision? And when I say in camera, obviously, you talked about redacting, but however it is done, it has to be sufficient to understand where the conflicts may come while, in fact, protecting the privacy—necessary privacy of judges.

Mr. GEYH. Right. And I would—there is a Judicial Conference committee on financial disclosures that I assume would be able to help with that, but yes.

Mr. ISSA. Now, currently, each circuit is the highest authority for whether a judge is competent. Isn't that correct?

Mr. GEYH. Competent to—oh, in terms of having a conflict?

Mr. ISSA. No, if a judge becomes unable——

Mr. GEYH. The disability provisions.

Mr. ISSA. Yeah, under disability, it is decided——

Mr. GEYH. The circuits control that.

Mr. ISSA. And constitutionally, what basis is there for a circuit to decide it when, in fact, the Constitution only gives authority to the Supreme Court?

Mr. GEYH. What is the constitutional authority for the legislation that provides for that, you mean?

Mr. ISSA. Well, what is the constitutional basis for putting it in the circuit rather than holding some level of responsibility? In other words, do we have—have we written statutes that negate the ultimate responsibility of nine men and women on the court?

Mr. GEYH. Well, if we are talking about the competence issue, I think that—I mean, the way I look at it is the 1980 legislation provided for a circuit-based disciplinary and competence standard that dates back to 1939.

Mr. ISSA. Okay. And I will be brief with the last two wrap—quick questions. One, currently, there is no transparency as to that. In other words, you really don't know whether somebody is being considered for either their technical competence, their health competence, or their ethical competence.

Mr. GEYH. In the early stages of the process, it is not. That is right.

Mr. ISSA. And lastly, currently, there is no requirement for physical or mental evaluations of judges even into their 70's, 80's, and 90's?

Mr. GEYH. Not that I am aware of.

Mr. ISSA. Thank you.

I now recognize the Ranking Member for his questions.

Mr. NADLER. Thank you, Mr. Chairman. I have several questions. Before I ask them, I ask unanimous consent that a statement from our colleague, Mr. Connolly of Virginia, be entered into the record regarding his legislation, the "Cameras in the Courtroom Act," which would require television coverage of the Supreme Court, along with a copy of the bill.

Mr. ISSA. Without objection, so ordered.

Statement for the Record
Submitted by Mr. Connolly of Virginia

The Washington Post, in an editorial published on February 8, 2017, stated that the federal judiciary's "role of administering justice and interpreting the law makes the judicial branch different from the political branches, but no less important to Americans who deserve to see — literally — how their government functions."

The Supreme Court currently allocates roughly 50 seats for the general public to view open proceedings. As you well know, the daily proceedings of Congress, both floor debate and committee hearings, are televised and available to all Americans through CSPAN. This dichotomy across equal branches of our federal government does a disservice to informed public debate.

The lack of transparency creates a perception of secrecy unworthy of the third branch of our government. It also limits the public and the media to one-dimensional and sometimes distorted views of the Justices' actions because court transcripts cannot provide the public and the media with the verbal intonations, body language, and other cues that can help interpret meaning and provide clarity.

That is why I introduced H.R. 464, the Cameras in the Courtroom Act, with my colleague Judge Ted Poe. Our bill would direct the Supreme Court to allow television coverage of all open proceedings unless a majority of justices agree that doing so would violate the due process rights of one or more parties before the court.

Our nation's highest court is not some "mystical priesthood" that can operate outside of the public view. Despite what some might say, cameras wouldn't diminish the Court to a "Judge Judy" episode. But they would bring accountability and transparency to the judicial branch, something the public overwhelmingly supports.

Sunshine – even in the Supreme Court – remains the best disinfectant against those who might feel that the black robe of life-tenure grants them permanent immunity from accountability for their words and opinions.

I hope this committee will be a champion of transparency and consider the Cameras in the Courtroom Act for markup.

———————

115TH CONGRESS
1ST SESSION

H. R. 464

To permit the televising of Supreme Court proceedings.

IN THE HOUSE OF REPRESENTATIVES

JANUARY 12, 2017

Mr. CONNOLLY (for himself, Mr. POE of Texas, Ms. CASTOR of Florida, Mr. CICILLINE, Mr. COHEN, Mr. LYNCH, Mr. NADLER, Ms. NORTON, Mr. QUIGLEY, and Mr. YARMUTH) introduced the following bill; which was referred to the Committee on the Judiciary

---

A BILL

To permit the televising of Supreme Court proceedings.

1   *Be it enacted by the Senate and House of Representa-*

2 *tives of the United States of America in Congress assembled,*

3 **SECTION 1. SHORT TITLE.**

4   This Act may be cited as the "Cameras in the Court-

5 room Act".

6 **SEC. 2. AMENDMENT TO TITLE 28.**

7   (a) IN GENERAL.—Chapter 45 of title 28, United

8 States Code, is amended by adding at the end the fol-

9 lowing:

2

1 **"§ 678. Televising Supreme Court proceedings**

2   "The Supreme Court shall permit television coverage

3 of all open sessions of the Court unless the Court decides,

4 by a vote of the majority of justices, that allowing such

5 coverage in a particular case would constitute a violation

6 of the due process rights of one or more of the parties

7 before the Court.".

8   (b) CLERICAL AMENDMENT.—The chapter analysis

9 for chapter 45 of title 28, United States Code, is amended

10 by adding at the end the following:

"678. Televising Supreme Court proceedings.".

○

Mr. ISSA. And we will not take that as an endorsement of the alternate legislation, I trust.

Mr. NADLER. No, no, no, just as a reference. Thank you.

Mr. Osterreicher, it has been estimated that between the live stream on YouTube, Facebook Live, and simulcast on the cable networks, more than a million people tuned in to listen to the Ninth Circuit's oral arguments in the executive order case. Do you think that the ability to listen to the arguments without any news filter helps people counter the President's assertions or judge the validity of the President's assertions about the integrity of those proceedings?

Mr. OSTERREICHER. I think it is critical that people in—as I said, in this day and age of alternative facts and accusations of fake news against the media, that the people have an opportunity to see and hear for themselves how government is conducted in all three branches. Unfortunately, what we have seen is, in the judicial branch, that has not always been available, at least at the Federal level.

Mr. NADLER. Well, here it wasn't the media's characterization. It was the President's characterization of the hearing as terrible and horrible and so forth. And do you think that the fact that over a million people at least heard the audio stream helped counter that?

Mr. OSTERREICHER. It is a much more direct form of democracy where people can see and hear for themselves, just as our Framers envisioned being able to, you know, stop by a court on their way about their daily activities. Unfortunately, these days, that can't happen, but we do have the capability of that type of communication through audiovisual coverage.

Mr. NADLER. Thank you.

Now, the argument before the Ninth Circuit was a very high-profile case, obviously, and on rare occasions, the Supreme Court has released audio of high-profile cases within minutes of the arguments' completion instead of at the end of the week, as is the normal practice. Is there any rational distinction between how the Supreme Court handles high-profile cases and how it handles less newsworthy cases?

Mr. OSTERREICHER. I don't think that there should be. I think that they should develop some standard practices. In terms of releasing, they have only done that once. Most of the time, even in high-profile cases, in the two that I mentioned last year, they still said that, in a very terse statement, they would stand by their Friday release. And as most people know, Friday is not exactly the best day to get people's attention when they are trying to start their weekend.

Mr. NADLER. It is a dump day. But is there any rational distinction between the cases, other than that they were high profile, where the Supreme Court released the audio transcript quickly and most cases where they didn't?

Mr. OSTERREICHER. I don't think that there really should be. Again——

Mr. NADLER. Should be. But is there—is there a rational distinction that you can make that said: Well, here the Supreme Court said yes, but there, they said no for the following reason?

Mr. OSTERREICHER. No.

Mr. NADLER. There is no rational distinction here.

Mr. OSTERREICHER. Not as far as I can see.

Mr. NADLER. When the Supreme Court has released audio more quickly, have we witnessed any ill effects?

Mr. OSTERREICHER. No. I mean, it is an appellate review, so we are not looking at somebody's Sixth Amendment rights coming into play as we might in a trial court.

Mr. NADLER. That is why my bill doesn't include trial courts.

Mr. OSTERREICHER. I understand.

Mr. NADLER. One of the criticisms of bringing cameras into the courtroom that we hear most often is that the lawyers or judges may play to the cameras. Are you aware that this has occurred in any of the courts that participated in the Judicial Conference's pilot program?

Mr. OSTERREICHER. Not that I am aware of. And as a matter of fact, in that 10-year experiment in New York, I think the most telling statistic is the fact in the tens, if not hundreds of thousands of cases that were heard, not one appeal was taken in a criminal court case or in any case based on the fact that someone didn't get a fair trial under the Sixth Amendment because——

Mr. NADLER. In those——

Mr. OSTERREICHER [continuing]. Of the fact that there was a camera in the court.

Mr. NADLER. In those trials—in that trial situation, I suppose you would have to call it, are you aware of any allegations by anyone that any—that any hearing was affected by playing to the cameras?

Mr. OSTERREICHER. No, there has always been that speculation, but——

Mr. NADLER. Speculation. But any allegation that in that case this is what happened?

Mr. OSTERREICHER. None that I am aware of.

Mr. NADLER. Thank you.

And, Mr. Bruce, you have given a lot of careful thought to various ways that you believe PACER could be improved, both from a technical standpoint and ways to enhance public access to the documents contained in PACER. Have you had the opportunity to share your views with the administrative office of the courts?

Mr. BRUCE. No, I have not, sir.

Mr. NADLER. Oh. I was going to ask if they were receptive to your recommendations, but obviously, you haven't shared it with them.

Have you asked for the ability to share it with them?

Mr. BRUCE. I have not.

Mr. NADLER. Is there a reason for that or——

Mr. BRUCE. I am, to be honest with you, sir, fairly new to the issue. I have monitored it for years. It has not been—it has not been something to which I have paid deep attention until recently.

Mr. NADLER. And finally, what sort of ability does the public have to comment on PACER, if any?

Mr. BRUCE. None that I am aware of.

Mr. NADLER. Thank you. I yield back.

Mr. ISSA. I thank the gentleman.

We now recognize the Chairman of the full Committee, the gentleman from Virginia, Mr. Goodlatte.

Mr. GOODLATTE. Thank you, Mr. Chairman.

Mr. Geyh, in cases of alleged misconduct, this Committee has deferred to the Judiciary Committee, in some instances, for an initial investigation before its potential referral to us for further action, including the possibility of impeachment. Does the judicial branch operate in an efficient manner when it is conducting its investigations?

Mr. GEYH. Much more so. I think that this Committee lit a fire under the judiciary about 10, 15 years ago when this Committee reached the point of actually considering the impeachment of Judge Real. And part of it was to say: Look, if you are not going to do your job, we are going to have to jump in. And that, I think, resulted in some very positive things, including some upgrades to the judicial disciplinary process.

I now feel as though they are taking it seriously. I think that this kind of oversight is critical to maintain that. But yes, I do think that they are doing a much better job than they were if I were testifying 15 years ago.

Mr. GOODLATTE. I generally agree with that. I have had experience handling two impeachments of Federal district court judges. In one of those instances, I am not sure that the Committee would have had the wherewithal to proceed without the preliminary investigative work that was done by the, I believe in that case it was the Fifth Circuit Court of Appeals.

The Justice Department declined to prosecute in that case, and it left us in a situation where we really had to develop our own case. We had four Articles of Impeachment. In the end, the Senate voted to convict that judge in all four instances. And I would give a lot of credit to the work that was initially done by the Fifth Circuit to lay the groundwork and provide information to us that was the foundation for our building a case.

However, I also recall that in that case there were a number of judges that did not believe that the offenses that had been committed by that judge were indeed impeachable offenses. And so I am wondering if this process, the way it is laid out today, puts the judiciary in an awkward situation where people who work with each other on a regular basis are called upon to pass judgment upon those same members of that same circuit of the judiciary. I am wondering if you have any observations about that?

Mr. GEYH. Well, I am not sure if you are talking about Judge Porteous.

Mr. GOODLATTE. I am talking about Judge Porteous.

Mr. GEYH. I was an expert witness for the prosecution in that case.

I differentiate in my own mind between conduct that judges may think is bad behavior warranting discipline and conduct that is so bad that it warrants impeachment. And I felt as though that was an example of the system working as it should because they worked it through the pipeline and ultimately recommended that impeachment be taken.

The Real case that I talked about before is more of a case where I think it was dysfunctional, because then the system ground out for years in the disciplinary phase without the public having adequate notice.

I do think—what you are calling attention to is the inherent problem of judges judging their own, and that is an inherent problem. And to my way of thinking, the way we address that problem best is by keeping, you know, feet to the fire in a limited way by basically having hearings like this in which we bring the judges forward and say, what is the process, how does it work, tell us how it works, and whether we are getting adequate transparency at what points in the process so that we can look at it and say this is good.

The one last point I will make is that Congress abandoned meaningful impeachment investigation in the 1940's because it is bloody exhausting, that they waited for someone else, either a prosecution or the judicial branch to go first. I think that is preferable, given how much work this body has, if we can manage to make that doable.

Mr. GOODLATTE. I take it then, however, that you think we should have another panel or another hearing in which we invite judges themselves to come and talk about these same issues that you are——

Mr. GEYH. I think so. I think that is important, yeah.

Mr. GOODLATTE [continuing]. Addressing here today, and I agree with you.

Mr. Osterreicher, some have expressed concern about sensitive information being made public if cameras are allowed into the courtroom. How can sensitive information best be protected when cameras are present?

Mr. OSTERREICHER. Well, I think that every legislation that I have seen really relies on the discretion of the trial court judge. He or she should be the final arbiter as to what happens in his or her courtroom.

At the appellate level, I think, you know, there is a number, in all the briefings, if something needs to be redacted, that is fine, but I can't imagine, during an oral argument at the appellate level, that we would see that sensitive information.

So at the trial court level, once again, I think that should be in the discretion of the presiding judge.

Mr. NADLER. Would the gentleman yield? Would the gentleman yield for a second.

Mr. GOODLATTE. Yeah, I will be happy to yield.

Mr. NADLER. And in any event, if that problem exists, that problem exists with the audio which is released now. The camera doesn't really add or detract from that problem.

Mr. GOODLATTE. I thank the gentleman for his comments. I thank the witness, and I yield back.

Mr. ISSA. I thank the gentleman.

And we now go to the gentleman from Michigan, Mr. Conyers.

Mr. CONYERS. Thank you so much.

I want to go back to the cameras in the courtroom for just a minute. Some believe that cameras in the courtroom could heighten the level of and the potential threats to Federal judges, particularly those proceedings involving highly controversial matters.

Mr. Osterreicher, how do you feel about that?

Mr. OSTERREICHER. Well, I think it is very difficult to put the genie back in the bottle. As we have seen from the internet, if you do a search, you can usually find somebody's image with their name. The last time that I testified before the Subcommittee, that issue was raised as well by the Federal trial court judge who was also one of the witnesses. I had never seen her before but was able to, once again, google her name and come up with lots of images of her.

So the fact is that if somebody is testifying in court, that their image will be shown, I think—I certainly understand the concerns of the jurists there. But again, in terms of the presiding justice, if there is a security issue with one of the witnesses, then that judge has the ability to decide that that video not be recorded or broadcast.

Mr. CONYERS. Professor Geyh, in your testimony, you state that there are 25,000 judicial offices in the United States. All but nine, of whom are most visible and influential nine in the Nation, are not subject to a Code of Judicial Conduct. Should Congress consider legislation that requires the Supreme Court to promulgate a code of conduct applicable to itself?

Mr. GEYH. I think so. Steve Gillers and I wrote an op-ed last year in support of Mr. Murphy's bill that did just that. And you know, in a perfect world, the judiciary would quietly appoint a Committee and promulgate a code of its own based on the Code of Conduct for U.S. judges, but it hasn't done that. And I do think that if we are concerned about the legitimacy of the judiciary, we really ought to think seriously about insisting that they take that step.

Mr. CONYERS. And let me add this. Is it possible that President Trump's recent statements about the judiciary could cause citizens to lose faith in the rule of law and the judiciary, and why would that be a huge problem if that is so?

Mr. GEYH. In my view, sustained attacks not in the form of criticism of judicial decisions, not in the form of criticism of judges, but suggesting that the judiciary should not be respected because the judges are so-called because they are only deserving of respect if you—if they do what the President wants, over the long term, that can erode public confidence in the independent judiciary.

And let me just say that I am not a social scientist, but I follow a lot of social science about this, and the social scientists have drawn a line between talking about the courts as legal realists where they are influenced by their ideologies and so forth. The public understands that. Ninety percent of the public is cool with that. They understand how that works. It doesn't cause them to think twice about the legitimacy of the courts.

The line gets crossed when they are perceived as just politicians in robes. In other words, not just that these are honorable people who may be influenced by their backgrounds and experience, but they are politicians in robes. And the concern I have is when you are calling them just political, when you are saying they are so-called, when you are calling them disgraceful is that you run that risk, and at that point, I think you can—very quickly, the judiciary can fall like a house of cards if we lose that legitimacy.

Mr. CONYERS. Thank you so much. Is it possible then that President Trump's recent statements about the judiciary could cause citizens to lose faith in the rule of law and the judiciary?

Mr. GEYH. I would like to think that the American people are made of sterner stuff in the sense that if this persists, we have a serious problem. My hope is that the response to those attacks creates a public debate that allows for this problem to be neutralized. So I regard—I join conservative scholar Will Baude, who was in the Washington Post last weekend, saying these attacks are deadly serious. By themselves, I am not sure that they are going to diminish the legitimacy of the judiciary, but if gone unresponded to or uncorrected, they could.

Mr. CONYERS. My final question is to Director Bruce. What barriers should be removed that prevent the public from reading the opinions of the court, in your estimation?

Mr. BRUCE. The first and most important barrier is economic. It is the per page viewing fee. The second is a problem of sort of practical obscurity that has to do with the data in the system. So, for example, in PACER currently, it is actually not possible to retrieve, with any certainty, the author of a specific opinion. In other words, if you want to see all the opinions by Judge Smith, that cannot be done with complete confidence. And there are other metadata lacks we could point at, but that is the most striking one.

Mr. CONYERS. Thank you so much.

Thank you, Mr. Chairman.

Mr. ISSA. I thank the gentleman.

We now go to the gentleman from Pennsylvania, Mr. Marino.

Mr. MARINO. Thank you, Mr. Chairman.

Welcome, gentlemen, and let me get directly to the issue. Do any of you support cameras in the courtroom other than, other than appellate arguments? And start with you, Mr. Geyh.

Mr. GEYH. I support it only in appellate arguments. I support it in limited use in trial scenarios, carefully circumscribed to protect litigant rights.

Mr. MARINO. Professor Bruce?

Mr. BRUCE. I agree with Professor Geyh.

Mr. MARINO. Okay. Sir?

Mr. OSTERREICHER. I support them in all aspects of the judicial proceedings. For all these years, all of the concerns that have been expressed have been shown to just be speculative.

The last time the Supreme Court heard a case based on the fact that somebody claimed they didn't get a fair trial, due to cameras was 1981 in *Florida v. Chandler.*

So I think, again, under the discretion of the trial court judge, that cameras are absolutely crucial to allow the public to see what goes on in courtrooms.

Mr. MARINO. But sir, don't you think that speculation is something that really should not play a part in this, particularly in a criminal proceeding?

In a capital murder case for the person—the defendant, for the family members, who are sitting there because of the victim, anything that we can prevent from swaying a decision other than the facts before the jury, I think, is most paramount. Do you have a response?

Mr. OSTERREICHER. I believe having been in courtrooms, throughout that 10-year period and beyond, that the jury, the participants, are completely unaware of the fact that there are cameras.

And that was when there were actual personnel in the courtrooms. Now we have multiple cameras in this room. I think, for the most part, eventually, people get used to the fact that they are there. We're videotaped and photographed a dozen if not more times a day——

Mr. MARINO. Don't you think that a witness—a witness, particularly a child, would have reservations about testifying in front of a camera? Don't you think that—look, there's enough grandstanding in Congress before the cameras in hearings and on the floor. Can you imagine what would take place in a courtroom?

Mr. OSTERREICHER. Well, I kind of saw what took place in the courtroom during the O.J. Simpson trial.

Mr. MARINO. And that was a circus in and of itself. Even the judge—even the judge, in my opinion, spent too much time looking at the cameras as did defense and prosecution. This is a dangerous, dangerous area to get into.

I was a prosecutor for 18 years and a rule of law person, you know, and the last thing we need is speculation that, well, nothing will happen. What if something happens?

Mr. OSTERREICHER. But that in itself is speculation. I think, you know, in terms of——

Mr. MARINO. It's not a speculation as to whether a person's going to be executed, whether a victim or a victim's family is going to seek to receive justice.

I have no problem at the appellate level, but going into the courtroom is—it's just another entertainment to be turned into a circus, as we see now, particularly with video cameras, people with their cell phones. This is—we're treading on dangerous, dangerous area here as far as rights are concerned and the rule of law. I'll let you respond.

Mr. OSTERREICHER. I understand and respect your opinion. I think when you're talking about a child or a reluctant witness, once again, the trial court can decide whether or not——

Mr. MARINO. So who makes this determination? Every single judge? Who makes the determination? A panel of judges? You three? Us in Congress? Who sits down and determines what the guidelines are?

Mr. OSTERREICHER. I think that each judge in—that is presiding over that courtroom, just like they have to make rulings——

Mr. MARINO. Well, we have numerous—we have numerous, multiple decisions made as to whether there'll be a camera there or whether there will not be a camera there and nothing consistent. I think you understand my position on this. And I yield back the remainder of my time.

Mr. ISSA. Can I—would you yield to me?

Mr. MARINO. Certainly.

Mr. ISSA. I want to follow up on his question. In a criminal trial, you have somebody who is innocent until proven guilty. If you stream live even their testimony or their face, are you or are you not, in fact, making a public characterization? And is that something that's—and I know they do it in State court. Is that something that we must do, or is it something that we'd like to do?

And I think that's where the gentleman from Pennsylvania's question goes, where he looks at appellate and says, we could be onboard, because we don't have this question of innocent people, whether they're witnesses, plaintiffs, defendants.

So I would follow-up and just ask, is this something that would be nice to do, that you would like to do, or, in fact, is getting the appellate made universally available, including the Supreme Court, more likely to be something where the American people have a right to know, and there's less conflict involved?

Mr. OSTERREICHER. I would be happy to start anywhere. And if it's at the appellate level, I think there should be a rebuttable presumption that courtrooms are open and open to cameras. And then if there is something that can refute that, for whatever reason, at either the appellate level, the Supreme Court, or a trial court level, then that can be dealt with. But that's just something that I think the public has a right to see.

We've all, I think, are in agreement that courtrooms are open to the public, and kind of blaming the camera for the circus-like atmosphere that goes on sometimes inside and sometimes outside the courtroom, I think, is shooting the messenger.

The example that I would use at a Federal level is during the trial of the Oklahoma City bomber. There were cameras in the courtroom that were used to broadcast closed circuit TV so that people back home where the bombing took place could watch that. And, unfortunately, the public missed an opportunity to see a well-conducted trial by Judge Matsch there versus the circus that we saw in O.J.

Mr. ISSA. I appreciate that.

We now go to the gentleman from Georgia, Mr. Johnson, for 5 minutes.

Mr. JOHNSON OF GEORGIA. Thank you, Mr. Chairman, for holding this hearing.

And thank you, gentlemen, for being here today to testify.

Mr. Osterreicher, in Professor Geyh's remarks, his written remarks, and also his testimony, he lays out the principle that Federal judges derive their legitimacy from the respect that they command as a result of their personal competence, impartiality, independence, and integrity? Do you agree with that statement?

Mr. OSTERREICHER. I do.

Mr. JOHNSON OF GEORGIA. And how you about, Professor Bruce?

Mr. BRUCE. Yes, I do.

Mr. JOHNSON OF GEORGIA. And to maintain that respect that they command as a result of the perception of competence, impartiality, independence, and integrity, judges should make decisions according to the law, unclouded by personal bias or conflicts of interest. That's another statement that Professor Geyh makes in his written testimony.

Do you both agree with that as well?

Professor Bruce and Mr. Osterreicher?

Mr. OSTERREICHER. I do.

Mr. BRUCE. Yes, I do.

Mr. JOHNSON OF GEORGIA. And do you also agree that when the public perceives a lack of competence, impartiality, or bias in favor of one party against the other, then the integrity of the judicial branch is undermined?

Mr. BRUCE. Of course.

Mr. OSTERREICHER. Yes, but that's a more subjective view depending on your point of view then.

Mr. JOHNSON OF GEORGIA. Well, but judges should strive to avoid an appearance that they might be biassed in favor of one party?

Mr. OSTERREICHER. Absolutely.

Mr. JOHNSON OF GEORGIA. And this is the reason why judges, Federal judges, are bound by the code of conduct for United States judges—excuse me—for United States—yes, for the United States judges. Correct?

Mr. OSTERREICHER. Yes.

Mr. JOHNSON OF GEORGIA. Is to protect those ideals and to ensure that they abide by those ideals.

But it's troubling that U.S. Supreme Court justices are not bound by a—or by that code of conduct for United States judges.

Do you have the same bad feeling about that that I and Professor Geyh have, Mr. Osterreicher?

Mr. OSTERREICHER. I think that it should apply across the board to all the judges.

Mr. JOHNSON OF GEORGIA. You, Professor Bruce?

Mr. BRUCE. For what the opinion of a computer scientist is worth, yes, I do.

Mr. JOHNSON OF GEORGIA. Well, tell me, is there any reason why there is some uniqueness of the United States Supreme Court justices that would exempt them from some code of ethics or code of conduct?

And you've already answered that question, so let me—let me ask this: Professor Geyh, is there any reason—is there any constitutional basis that would prevent Congress from imposing upon the U.S. Supreme Court justices a rule that they abide by the code of conduct for United States judges, or that they write a code of conduct for themselves and abide by it?

Mr. GEYH. Steve Gillers and I are both of the opinion that the necessary and proper clause, coupled with the power to regulate the appellate jurisdiction of the Supreme Court, gives this body the power to insist on a code of conduct.

I think for those of us who are originalists, I think it's useful to know, you know, that the original Congress was happy to identify how many judges that would have to be on the Supreme Court, when they would sit, where they would sit. It made them get on horseback and run around the country.

And so against the backdrop of those early regulations, the idea that you would simply say, look, we want to make sure that our judiciary, as a condition of the appellate process, that our judges subscribe to basic ethical principles strikes me as being within the zone.

I'm not sure—there might be a counter. There may well be others who disagree, but I think there is congressional power for that.

Mr. JOHNSON OF GEORGIA. Thank you.

Mr. Osterreicher, do you agree with that?

Mr. OSTERREICHER. I absolutely do. I think that, unfortunately, I believe what we're seeing now is the Supreme Court promulgates its own rules. So that, I think, would be the explanation for why they don't have rules that are in line with the other justices.

Mr. JOHNSON OF GEORGIA. Well, I'm sure that justices, unlike judges, want to be judges of their own cases. And I think that whenever you have a justice that is solely responsible for judging an issue of recusal, then it diminishes the respect that people have for the court's perception of abiding by the law and being unbiassed, impartial, and all the rest.

And with that, I will yield back. Thank you.

Mr. ISSA. I thank the gentleman.

We now go to the gentleman from Idaho, Mr. Labrador.

Mr. LABRADOR. Thank you, Mr. Chairman. Pleased to be joining this Subcommittee and look forward to talking about this issue and many other issues about the Federal judiciary.

Mr. Osterreicher, I have a quick question. I appreciate your approach to transparency in the courtroom and the role that cameras and live streaming can play. I was actually a criminal defense attorney, and I practiced in Federal courts. I was also a law clerk in the Federal courts in Idaho, and I'm ambivalent and a little bit conflicted about having cameras.

Because I do see—you just gave the example of the O.J. Simpson trial and then you mentioned how unfortunate it was that another trial didn't have cameras because of how well it was conducted. But then that begs the question, was it properly conducted because there were no cameras in the——

Mr. OSTERREICHER. No, there were cameras, they just were closed circuit cameras.

Mr. LABRADOR. Correct. Correct. Because they knew that they weren't—it wasn't a nationally televised circus that they were presiding over. So that's the question that—and I'm not taking a position. That's the conflict that I have, because I have seen how it has had a deleterious effect on some trials, and I think the justice was not served in some of those trials.

Mr. OSTERREICHER. I think that, unfortunately, that atmosphere, in the O.J. trial, would have gone on with or without cameras. There was a whole lot more circus going on outside the courtroom when people—when both—all the parties went through the gauntlet of the media that was outside.

I think, once again, it really shows that if the public—and, for example, the civil trial that followed regarding Mr. Simpson, again, there were cameras there. It was broadcast, and people got to watch that trial. There wasn't a whole lot of commenting going on, a whole lot of spin as to what happened or what you just saw.

I think we need to give the public credit, just as we have for them listening to the oral arguments the other day in the Ninth Circuit to be able to see and hear for themselves what went on. And that will also——

Mr. LABRADOR. And I don't disagree with that. I have no problem with the oral argument in the Ninth Circuit. I actually enjoyed listening to it myself.

Do you believe that cameras should be allowed in all types of trial court proceedings, including criminal matters and preliminary matters addressed without a jury present?

Mr. OSTERREICHER. I do, once again, within the discretion of the presiding judge.

Mr. LABRADOR. How do you answer the concerns of those that suggest that broadcasting trials will have a chilling effect on whistleblowers and other possibly reluctant witnesses?

Mr. OSTERREICHER. Once again, I would say this has been unfounded speculation for, you know, scores of years already. And there's really no proof of that.

In the New York 10-year experiment, they did four different studies where they asked judges, parties, witnesses, prosecutors, lawyers, to fill out forms, and both the empirical and anecdotal data show exactly the opposite happened where cameras were in the courtroom.

Mr. LABRADOR. Professor Geyh, do you believe that the grounds for disqualification are well-stated in the statute?

Mr. GEYH. Pretty well, yeah. They are mostly uniform across the country at this point.

Mr. LABRADOR. To what extent, if any, have you seen or learned of attorneys using these sections of law to shop for more favorable judges?

Mr. GEYH. It happens, but it is a very risky gambit. In other words, I think the opposite is almost more likely the case. In other words, lawyers think long and hard before they're going to show up in front of a judge and point a finger in his face and say, you're too biassed to sit, because more likely than not, the judge will say no, and then they're going to have a case heard by a pissed off judge.

Mr. LABRADOR. So, hypothetically, should a judge's political leaning or proclivity for or against a certain political position be sufficient ground for disqualification?

Mr. GEYH. No.

Mr. LABRADOR. Your testimony recounts the procedural hurdles and resulting issues with employing section 144. Can Congress amend 144 so that attorneys could conceivably use it as a method for moving—of moving for disqualification of a judge?

Mr. GEYH. It could.

Mr. LABRADOR. How?

Mr. GEYH. How could they do it?

Mr. LABRADOR. Yes.

Mr. GEYH. I think that I would recommend——

Mr. LABRADOR. Well, what changes do you suggest?

Mr. GEYH. Well, I mean, I think I would borrow changes that are made in Alaska and Montana both have statutes, which essentially allows for substitution of judges. It's a one-time only—a one-time only arrangement in which a party can request a different judge without making the allegation that the judge was biassed. And it's judge shopping, but it's a one-shot deal.

And the word—you know, the word that I received when I was working this issue was that it cut way back on disqualification for cause later, so—and the people who use it like it. The people that don't resent it. The people who don't use it, sort of, worry that it creates this judge shopping thing.

But the people who use it, well, if that's one way to preserve public confidence in the courts by a one-shot only deal, it will work.

Mr. LABRADOR. Thank you.

I yield back my time.

Mr. ISSA. Did you mention also California has that——

Mr. GEYH. California—about 20 jurisdictions do, and most of them are in the West. And most of the ones that use it are pretty—are okay with it. Not all, but—I think mean, I think I've heard some judges complain, but it's the ones that don't use it that find it difficult to fathom.

Mr. ISSA. Thank you.

We now go to the gentleman from Florida, Mr. Deutch.

Mr. DEUTCH. Thank you, Mr. Chairman. Mr. Chairman, I have very mixed feelings about today's hearing. On the one hand, I agree——

Mr. ISSA. About the hearing or the subject matter?

Mr. DEUTCH. About the hearing and the subject matter. I do agree that there's a lot to be done and needs to be done to improve public access to the PACER service. As someone who has personally—has had the joy of muddling through PACER, I can see what a difference improvement would make, and I'm glad we're having the opportunity to talk about that.

Similarly, revisions to Federal court policy on cameras are long overdue as well. Policies prohibiting cameras in the courtrooms impose severe limitations on the public's ability to observe court proceedings, interpreting laws that can impact the daily activities of every American. These restrictive broadcasting policies shroud the Supreme Court, and Federal court proceedings in secrecy and raise questions in the minds of the public on the administration of justice.

You can walk into any State or Federal courtroom in America and see rows of benches or seats to accommodate public audiences interested in watching the legal proceedings. The U.S. Supreme Court also has public seating available to accommodate the lucky few courtroom seating for audiences recognizes and accommodates our Nation's long tradition of public court watching.

The U.S. Supreme Court and our Federal courts hear and consider some of the most important issues facing our country. The proceedings and the decisions issued from the proceedings by the Supreme Court and Federal courts impact every facet of lives of Americans. The Supreme Court and the Federal courts need to recognize and adapt to these changes to permit the next generation of court watchers' access to proceedings on important legal issues. Such changes should include permitting television broadcasting.

I've long supported the efforts of Mr. King, Mr. Nadler, and others in trying to open our Nation's courts to public access through cameras with appropriate protections for the parties and judicial discretion ever-sensitive matters. It's time that the Supreme Court and Federal court's practices change.

But I cannot help feeling the twinge of regret at the focus this week on judicial transparency and ethics when the executive branch had such glaring problems with both.

It doesn't take a constitutional law scholar to see that President Trump should not continue to have an ownership stake in the company that bears his name. His family's operation of the Trump Organization has already given foreign governments the opportunity to funnel improper payments through Trump hotels and golf courses and rental properties to curry favor with the Administration with no accountability to the American people.

The complete inadequacy of President Trump's approach to conflicts begs us here, the House Judiciary Committee, to investigate ethics violations of the President and his nominees. His choice to violate the Constitution and complete—and his complete disregard for the well-established norms followed by previous Administrations expose our democracy to potential foreign influence and to the risk that he will use the power of his office to divert the public good for his own private benefit.

These, Mr. Chairman, I would respectfully suggest, are the most pressing issues of transparency and ethics facing our country today.

But, since executive transparency and ethics falls outside the jurisdiction of the Subcommittee on the Courts, Intellectual Property and the Internet, and since this Committee as a whole seems fiercely determined to ignore our executive oversight responsibilities in the face of unprecedented threats by the Trump administration, I suppose the judicial transparency is the most we can hope for, and I am grateful for our witnesses for sharing their thoughts on this important topic today.

And with that, I yield back.

Mr. ISSA. The gentleman yields back.

With that, we go to the gentleman from Texas, Mr. Poe.

Mr. POE. Thank you, Chairman.

Thank you all for being here. During my other life, I was a proud judge in Texas for 22 years. I tried only felony cases, everything from stealing to killing and everything in between. And I was one of the first, if not the first, trial judge in Texas to allow cameras in the courtroom. We had a very structured system where we had to—it was very discreet. The jury never saw the camera.

The camera did not film the jury, did not film child witnesses, sexual assault witnesses, or any other witness that the lawyers did not agree should be filmed. And those that opposed that system, you know, said the world would end if we had cameras in the courtroom, where all lawyers would play to the cameras, and all of those things that—and no offense to the academics, but the academics were opposed to it, because they had never been in a courtroom and never had tried a case in their life, from either point of view.

But none of that happened. Lawyers don't play to the cameras. They play to the trier of fact, whether it's the court or the jury. And we tried very serious cases, including death penalty cases, and we allowed cameras to film those cases. And it worked, and it was great for not just the public, but for law students and their universities to see those cases tried from gavel to gavel.

And I'm a great fan of that, because we have the greatest judicial system in the world for determining guilt or innocence. No, it's not perfect, but it is the absolute best that anybody has ever come up

with. And why would we not want the world to see it? And the public is stuck with a 90-second sound bite on the news by what some
reporter thinks took place in the courtroom that day, whether it's
in a trial court or whether it's in the Supreme Court, or appellate
court, or a Federal District Court, because they are not permitted
to see what took place in that courtroom. And I think it is shame-
ful that the public cannot see that.

So I am absolutely in favor of cameras in the courtroom, cospon-
soring with Mr. Connolly a bill that would allow cameras in the Supreme Court unless the court decides due process would be violated. There are other bills. Mr. Nadler has a bill that's even more
progressive, if I could use that word—than——

Mr. NADLER. All right with me.

Mr. POE [continuing]. If it's all right with you, Mr. Nadler—than
just the Supreme Court to let Federal courts be open. I think that
the recent case of the—that was in Seattle, before a Federal court,
would have been a perfect example of allowing that case to be
heard with a camera in the courtroom and let the public see for
themselves, without having to rely on the news media's 90-second
sound bite, as to what took place in that courtroom.

Mr. SWALWELL. Would the gentleman yield?

Mr. POE. Yes.

Mr. SWALWELL. Judge, I appreciate your thoughts and personal
experience on this. Could you share what you did in the courtroom
to protect—if there was a sexual assault victim or a victim who had
been threatened by the defense? Because I share a lot of your be-
liefs here, but was wondering what you did in your personal experience presiding over the court to protect those victims?

Mr. POE. If there was a—reclaiming my time.

If there was a sexual assault victim, that victim was not televised in the courtroom. That was the rule. Sexual assault victims
are never televised. And only the audio sometimes was allowed, but
only by agreement of the prosecutor and the victim and, of course,
the defense attorney. But the video was never televised in those
cases.

And child witnesses—the same was true with a child witness,
never a child witness. Even if it was not a—the witness was not
a victim, the child witness was never televised as well.

And so we had certain rules. And the media abided by those
rules. We never had a problem with the media violating the rules.
They knew they—there were consequences. They might be in jail
if they violated the rules. We never had a problem with it.

So it worked out very well. We went through all of the so-called
problems, and I was impressed, really, how smoothly all of that
worked.

Mr. JOHNSON OF GEORGIA. Mr. Chairman, by unanimous consent
I'd ask that the gentleman be granted an additional minute to con-
clude his remarks.

Mr. ISSA. Without objection.

Mr. POE. I thank the Chairman.

Anyway, I will get to a question in a minute—in less than a
minute.

So it's just, I think, in this day and time, and has been said by
many people, that we show the world that the most important

court in the world, the Supreme Court of the United States, where you can go and sit—but you can't sit but 15 minutes until they kick you out and bring in another bunch of folks. Because that's their rule over there. You can't watch the whole trial unless you're on this side of the bar—that they get to see everything that takes place in the Supreme Court. I think it would be of tremendous benefit to law students to see that and to lawyers, God bless them, let them see what takes place before the Supreme Court and, of course, the public as well.

Mr. Osterreicher, would you agree with that—that scenario or not?

Mr. OSTERREICHER. Oh, I would absolutely agree. I commend you for your progressive attitude. I'm admitted to the Supreme Court. And we have filed amicus briefs in a number of cases. I've appeared for oral arguments in those cases, and I just sit there and shake my head at the fact that there's only about 300 people in that room that get to see what goes on in that courtroom. We're seeing people, you know, pay a lot of money for somebody to hold their place to get a spot in.

But in terms of the snippets, that's the other thing that was always a contention. Well, you're only going to show a small part of the trial or a 15-second sound bite. The fact is that nowadays with live streaming, with the fact that not only live streaming on the internet, but by broadcast websites, by print websites, you can have the public be able to see the whole trial for themselves. Yes, we'll still be relegated to a small part on the news, but right now the public has no other opportunity to see what goes on in the courtroom other than that snippet where cameras are allowed. In this case, with live streaming, I think that will be available for everybody to either watch live or watch later.

Mr. POE. I thank the Chairman for the extra time.

Mr. ISSA. You can thank Mr. Johnson.

Thank you. The gentleman yields back.

We now go to the gentleman from New York, Mr. Jeffries.

Mr. JEFFRIES. I thank the Chairman for yielding and for convening us here today.

I thank the panel for the information that you've presented for your expertise, for your presence here today. This certainly, is an otherwise important topic, although I would suggest that the timing of this hearing is a bit perplexing. There is a swamp of corruption that's percolating at 1600 Pennsylvania Avenue. The national security adviser has resigned in disgrace. Our national security has been placed in jeopardy as a result of the Trump administration continuing to play footsie with Vladimir Putin and the Russians. It's impossible to figure out where the Trump family business ends and the White House begins.

The President himself is a living, breathing, conflict of interest. Seventeen different intelligence agencies have concluded that the Russians interfered with our election in order to help Donald Trump, and yet, we're here today talking about the PACER system. It just seems to me that there are more pressing issues related to the existential threat that this Administration presents to our democracy that we could be spending our time on.

Now, we have a President who is in the illegitimacy business. He peddles illegitimacy with all the viciousness of a street corner dealer. He spent 5 years perpetrating the racist lie that Barrack Obama was not born in the United States of America, trying to un‑ dermine the legitimacy of a duly elected and re‑elected President. He regularly attacks the legitimacy of the news media, the so‑ called fourth estate, which is essential to the constitutional fabric of our democracy. It's why we have a First Amendment. He has questioned the legitimacy of the intelligence agencies that now re‑ port to him. I wonder why? And he's also gone after the legitimacy of the judiciary.

And so to the extent we've got the expertise available on this panel to deal with that issue, Professor Geyh, let me ask a question. You state that the survival of our courts depends upon the perceived legitimacy with the people in this country that they serve. Is that correct?

Mr. GEYH. Yes.

Mr. JEFFRIES. And is that largely because members of the judiciary are appointed and they're not elected and, therefore, they derive any respect and legitimacy that they have from the factors that you've set forth as it relates to their competence, integrity, and independence?

Mr. GEYH. In part. I mean, part of it also is that every branch of government, really, does have the power to bring the other branches of government to their knees unless they believe in it. And to the extent we lose faith in the judiciary, there's no incentive not to abuse the other branches.

And so part of it is that the judiciary is uniquely vulnerable, because they aren't elected and don't have that reservoir of legitimacy from the electorate. But the other part of it is that in the absence of that legitimacy, the President and the Congress, both, can essentially delegitimize the judiciary themselves.

Mr. JEFFRIES. Donald Trump recently attacked a member of the Article III judiciary as a so‑called judge. Is that correct?

Mr. GEYH. Correct.

Mr. JEFFRIES. What exactly is a so‑called judge in your view?

Mr. GEYH. The reason I look at that as different than just robust criticism, it is implied—it implies that this is not a judge at all. This is someone masquerading as a judge, who is undeserving of our respect. And when you combine that with the statement later that if they want our respect, they will simply do what we want them to do, that tells me that I don't want an independent branch of government. I want someone who will simply do my wishes. And that worries me. That to me, delegitimizes the judiciary as a separate and independent branch of government.

Mr. JEFFRIES. It's amazing to me that we have a President who was helped by the Russians in terms of his election. The FBI director interfered in an unprecedented fashion. He benefited from the fake news industry throughout the election. He didn't win the popular vote. He lost the popular vote. A majority of the Americans didn't vote for him. They voted against him.

The Administration is now shrouded in scandal, and he calls an Article III member of the judiciary a so‑called judge. It's shameless, and this Committee needs to do something about these independent attacks on the judiciary.

I yield back.

Mr. ISSA. If the gentleman would yield?

Mr. JEFFRIES. Certainly.

Mr. ISSA. I'm going to associate myself with one part of what you just said, and that is that I don't believe we should ever use terms about judges that question their competence or integrity in—on this Committee unless we have a reason or anywhere else.

I will say that perhaps we all should entertain not delegitimizing the other branches except where we have a specific claim and in that venue. But I do want to share my—appreciation that we do need to all raise the standard of how we deal with the court, how we refer to differences, and how we believe something should have been decided or how they believe it.

I want to share that, because I think that—although I didn't necessarily associate with everything you said, I think it's important that this Committee, as we look at judicial responsibility, that we not disparage the court, which as you say, has generally done an extremely good job of delivering honest representation through the Federal court system.

I thank you.

Mr. JEFFRIES. I thank the Chairman for his remarks.

Mr. ISSA. Thank you.

We now go to Mr. Biggs, who has been patiently waiting.

And I want to apologize to you. I got a mixed signal, so you, actually, should have been before Mr. Poe, but I'm sure he appreciates your indulgence. Thank you.

Mr. BIGGS. Thanks, Mr. Chairman. And Mr. Poe can go before me any time he wants.

And I appreciate the subject for the hearing today, and I appreciate those who are here on this panel testifying today. I appreciate you being here.

You know, what I find interesting is that tensions, actually, between the three separate branches of our government are nothing new. Indeed they've been present in America since its inception. In fact, the very famous first case that laid the foundation for judicial review, Marbury versus Madison, arose specifically because of that tension between the executive branch and the judicial branch at that time.

So I think it's interesting to be—hear folks be critical of the current executive because of comments that he made with regard to the separate coequal branch of government. But it's not new, these types of discussions, whether it be Andrew Jackson or Thomas Jefferson or FDR's idea of packing a court, increasing the number of justices so you can get a desired outcome. This kind of tension is not new. It is as old as the republic is.

Mr. SWALWELL. Would the gentleman yield?

Mr. BIGGS. I haven't finished my statement yet. I'd like to finish my statement.

Mr. SWALWELL. Would you yield after?

Mr. BIGGS. I'm not yielding yet, so hold your question.

Additionally, when we look at the Article III branch of particularly the Federal judges here that we're talking about, many refer to them as being lifetime appointments, but in fact, that is only the de facto arrangement that has emerged and evolved over time. The actual language of Article III, section 1 says that they will hold their offices during good behavior.

And so, really, what we're talking about today, when I hear the testimony—and I appreciate it, because we're talking, really, in my opinion, about transparency and getting—having practiced law and having tried many cases, there is a certain mystery that kind of shrouds what goes on in the courts, and whether it's the broadcasting of court cases, whether it is the idea of making the PACER system more accessible to the public, whether we're talking about the ethical determination and processes within the courts themselves, I think those are really important issues to be sitting and discussing today.

And that's why I'm grateful that you're here and grateful for the Chairman for organizing and conducting this Committee hearing today.

So my question would be—for Professor Geyh is: As we look at this, what do you see are the real checks for the legislative branch on the judicial branch?

Mr. GEYH. The checks include the 100-ton gun, as it's so-called, is impeachment. You do have a check. You control the judiciary's budget. You control the lower court's jurisdiction. You are enabled by virtue of the fact that you have the discretion to establish courts that implies a lot of regulatory authority over things like a disciplinary process. And so because you can, theoretically, disestablish courts, you can regulate them in between. And so—and so there are all kinds of powers that can be used.

And, you know, getting back to the point you made before, I think it's an important point to recognize, that there's very little new under the sun, but that it's also true that we have a constitutional crises every now and then. That's not precedent for it being a good thing, it's just a precedent for it happening.

And one of the great things about our system of democracy, I think, is that we have—we know when to hold them and when to fold them. We know when to stay our hand and when to get aggressive. And I think that having all of these powers used wisely has kept us going as long as it has.

Mr. BIGGS. Thank you. And I—thank you, Professor Geyh. And I agree with you that there are a series of checks that the legislative branch has, and I'm not sure that we exercise those too often. But I think the discussion today with regard to disciplinary process that needs to be put in place, and maybe we discuss that with the U.S. Supreme Court itself, I think that is integral to exercising the article empowers—the checks against the courts itself.

Mr. GEYH. Fair point. Certainly, the inquiry is a fair one, yes. Mr. BIGGS. So in line with that, when we start looking at transparency.

And I think I'm just about out of time, but, Mr. Osterreicher, I was going to ask you, I want to know how we get access to the broadcast, and if that—in the 10-year study in New York, how was that made available?

Because it seems to me that as you're broadcasting, you are creating a separate record that is going to be relevant to any kind of appellate procedures when you're videotaping and recording lower court proceedings.

Mr. OSTERREICHER. Well, I think right now what we're seeing, at least at the Federal level during the pilots, is that they were operating the equipment rather than the media. So that becomes part of their——

In the Ninth Circuit, they have their own YouTube site. I would assume that they are retaining those records as public records. During the 1987 to 1997 10-year experiment, it was prior to live streaming, and, really, the only time you would get anything was—was that broadcast unless you're actually recording videotape of it as well for later broadcasts.

Mr. BIGGS. Thank you, Mr. Chairman.

Mr. ISSA. I thank the gentleman.

We now go to the also very patient, Mr. Swalwell of California.

Mr. SWALWELL. Thank you, Chairman, for this important hear- ing.

And I will go back to the gentleman, Mr. Biggs, and ask—and I would yield to him, do you agree with Judge Gorsuch that it was demoralizing for President Trump to call the judge in Washington a so-called judge?

Mr. BIGGS. Mr. Chairman, I will take the time.

Thank you so much for yielding time to me.

On that specific issue, I don't know what—apparently, Judge Gorsuch was demoralized. I don't know who else might have been demoralized. I don't know anybody else who might have been demoralized when Members of Congress say this President's——

Mr. SWALWELL. I'll reclaim my time, and I'll ask again, do you believe that it's demoralizing to call a judge a so-called judge? And I'll yield to the gentleman.

Mr. BIGGS. Thank you. And hearkening back to my trial court days, I'll say that I'm not sure that's relevant to anything what I specifically think on this. But you're asking a really broad question, and so I will tell you that I think that there are probably some judges that are more sensitive than others.

Mr. SWALWELL. I'll reclaim my time.

Mr. BIGGS. Some may be demoralized and some may not be, I don't know.

Mr. SWALWELL. I was a trial court prosecutor and look forward to working with the gentleman on this issue, but I guess I'll ask Mr. Geyh, you said, "We believe in the tripartite system of government that our Founders frame. We believe that the checks and balances that systems provide and the role that a strong separate and independent judiciary plays in keeping the executive and legislative branch in check."

So I guess I'd ask each person: Do you believe that calling a Federal District Court judge a so-called judge is respectful or disrespectful?

Mr. Osterreicher?

Mr. OSTERREICHER. I'm not sure that I'm going to be the one qualified for this. The only analogy I will draw is, this weekend I judged a moot court contest for law students, I was the presiding judge. I called myself the so-called judge only because I wasn't one. So I think using that reference to an actual judge is—certainly, calls into question why anyone would do that.

Mr. SWALWELL. Sure.

Mr. Bruce, respectful or disrespectful?

Mr. BRUCE. I would consider it, again, for what the opinion of a computer scientist is worth, I would consider it disrespectful.

Mr. SWALWELL. Thank you.

And Mr. Geyh?

Mr. GEYH. My testimony would suggest yeah, I don't think it's respectful.

Mr. SWALWELL. And how about your home State judge, Judge Curiel, being referred to as not being able to be impartial because of being a Mexican American?

Mr. GEYH. He's actually an alum of our law school as well. My concern there—I mean, to be clear, I'm less concerned about whether you're respectful than I am whether you are attacking the integrity of the court itself. And when you're implying that someone is incapable of rendering impartial justice because of the color of their skin, I think you've got trouble. That's more than disrespectful.

I think, similarly, calling someone so-called, I mean, it's a snippet. It's a tweet, but it's what we have to work with. It's trouble. I'm not going to go so far as to say it's the end of the world, but it is indicative of a larger problem that attacks the legitimacy of the court, and that's what worries me.

Mr. SWALWELL. Thank you. I want to go to the purpose—one of the purposes of the hearing. And after practicing in trial courts for 7 years, I've given a lot of thought to the O.J. trial. I was 13-years-old as I watched that unfold, and just like most of America, could not believe that he was acquitted. But as time passed by and as I spent time in a courtroom and I watched the recent documentaries—Mr. Osterreicher, do you think that—and this is quite an existential question, I guess, but do you think had there been cameras on the streets for the police officers of Los Angeles in the years leading up to the O.J. trial, do you think that would have actually been more informative, and that would have held them to account rather than folks blaming the cameras in the courtroom as being the reason that he was acquitted? Do you understand the question?

Mr. OSTERREICHER. I'm not quite sure I do.

Mr. SWALWELL. If the police officers had body cameras, and there was more transparency on those officers at that time, do you think that may have been more helpful and brought them into account? Because it seems to me that it wasn't the cameras in the courtroom that poisoned the jury, that it was really that there weren't cameras in the streets and that police officers in Los Angeles weren't being held accountable and their credibility was devastating.

Mr. OSTERREICHER. I think it may, but the fact was that most officers that responded to that crime scene were detectives. And at least as we see it now, only patrol officers are wearing body cams. So I think even if the program was fully implemented, I highly doubt that those detectives would have be wearing body cams. But, certainly, it would have helped to see who went where and did what with evidence collection.

Mr. SWALWELL. Thank you.

Mr. ISSA. Would the gentleman yield?

Mr. SWALWELL. Yes.

Mr. ISSA. I want to engage in a quick colloquy, because—do you think that, perhaps, politicians have gotten in the habit of—that extends between each other and then, you know, flows over into Article III?

You weren't here, but when I came to Congress, it was popular for many people to say that President Bush was an appointed not an elected President. Many people didn't come to his inauguration for that reason.

Obviously, here, today, we had a Member on the dais cite delegitimizing President Trump because he didn't win a majority, and because of "Russia" getting him the election. Is it, perhaps, just a spillover, and is it something that all of us, executive branch and here in the House and Senate, need to get out of the habit of delegitimizing ourselves, and thus, spilling over into Article III? I just wonder if you thought about that.

Mr. SWALWELL. Reclaiming my time. And I appreciate the question.

I guess the prosecutor in me says, just stick to the evidence. If you follow the evidence, you'll find the truth.

I yield back.

Mr. ISSA. The gentleman ends with a good yield back.

We now go to the gentlelady from California, Ms. Lofgren.

Ms. LOFGREN. Thank you, Mr. Chairman.

I, actually, agree that it seems a little out of body to be discussing the PACER system when the national security adviser resigned and people are questioning what did the President know and when did he know it. But that's what we're doing here, and so that's what I would like to pursue, which is the PACER system.

Professor Bruce, 10 years ago there was a pretty comprehensive privacy audit that academics performed on the PACER system, and they found that there were Social Security numbers included in the records. The audits were sent to the 31 district courts, administrative office of the courts, judicial conference, and the like. However, it's my understanding that despite those findings, you still have Social Security numbers scattered throughout the PACER system.

The technology of the systems is a little bit bulky, and I'm wondering if you have observations on what steps could be taken to redact sensitive information in the system or whether we might be well-advised to take up some of the private sector offers to take the data and maybe use better technology and as a condition of doing that, providing it for free to the public to redact sensitive information?

Mr. BRUCE. Let me make four points, actually, around the whole privacy issue. This is one of the places that has suffered the most from the inability to do comprehensive research across the entire system. If there were bulk access to the data, you would certainly have a lot better eyes on what was going on there.

Secondly, just as with the problems of privacy that surround cameras in the courts, this is a problem that's unevenly distributed across the courts, so it's sort of—sort of hard to know where to look.

We know from experience that a lot of this stuff can be very easily dealt with in software. It's been done in other jurisdictions. Mostly on something like Social Security numbers, that's going to be an easy problem to solve, because they are very easy to identify. There are harder problems and some that are completely insoluable. As for example, when you have a victim of domestic violence named as a 39-year-old school teacher from Gordon, Nebraska where there is maybe one 39-year-old school teacher. That, you're never going to get rid of.

In smaller jurisdictions in Canada and Australia, this has been done successfully with automation or more accurately automated support for some editorial redaction for a considerable period of time, at least 10 years or 15 in the case of Canada, shorter time in Australia. Should we take outside offers to do that? Yes, if they've got the technology, absolutely.

Ms. LOFGREN. Let me ask you something that's always bothered me. You can get some documents for free, but you have to create an account, and the account actually asks for your full name, your address, your phone number, your email address, your date of birth. It seems to me rather intrusive to have to provide all that information to get access to data that, really, the public should have.

Mr. BRUCE. That seems intrusive to me, too.

Ms. LOFGREN. I think—you know, what I'm interested in, Mr. Chairman, from this hearing is what steps we might take to recommend changes in this system.

First, I don't think we're ever going to get the technology upgrades we want in the current system. I think we ought to aggressively and systematically pursue private sector options that would allow free access to this data that is not—that provides adequate privacy protections for individuals whose presence is revealed in the documents and that provides it on a basis that is not intrusive for the public that should have every right to see this information. Mr.

BRUCE. If I may, this circles back a bit to the question that Mr. Nadler asked me earlier. If you look at the 2015 report from the AO on development of the NextGen system, it was actually a journal article that was published by the two senior designers, it's very clear from that that very, very little consideration was given to, really, any outside source of information beyond the judges who were—who were serving on the, you know, sort of, the media customer committee.

And that, in fact, the AO completely dismissed the recommendations of Mider Corporation, which is a very well-respected consulting group for this kind of judicial administration.

So I don't think I—I agree with you. I don't think we could expect a good deal of receptivity from the AO.

Ms. LOFGREN. Well, I would just say, I respected the judges for their insight into the law more than I respect the judges for their technology expertise.

And I would yield back.

Mr. NADLER. Mr. Chairman——

Mr. ISSA. Yes. For what purposes does the gentleman seek to be recognized?

Mr. NADLER. Mr. Chairman, I ask unanimous consent that the gentlelady from Texas, who is a Member of the full Committee but not of the Subcommittee, be permitted to ask questions?

Mr. ISSA. Without objection, so ordered.

The gentlelady from Texas is recognized.

Ms. JACKSON LEE. Let me thank the Ranking Member and the Chairman for their extended courtesies for a very important hearing.

And thank you, gentlemen, for your testimony but also for your advocacy.

I am going to follow a certain line of questioning, but let me give a question for a premise upon which it is based. I happen to be a member of the Bar. Sometimes we humorously ask which one, but I'm a member of the Bar and came through law school at the time that this was of great high honor.

And the whole idea of the sanctity of the Constitution and the strength of the Constitution was very much enshrined, if you will, in our law school, but more importantly, it was a document that we held with the highest of esteem and thought as we graduated we were going to be advocates, the single sponsors of the value of the Constitution to the American public or to our immediate constituencies, and at that time, we were not elected persons but just those who had graduated from law school.

With that in mind, Professor Geyh, I would like to go on a line of questioning that the other gentlemen made comment on, but I know that the issues that they are advocating I am very much familiar with, and I believe in their advocacy.

The good news about what has happened over the last couple of weeks has been the increased, by the American public, of understanding civics, understanding their government, understanding what role their government plays. And I've enjoyed speaking about the three branches of government; the judiciary, the legislature, and the executive which by the Constitution three equal branches of government. I love saying that.

We saw one episode with President Nixon in the Saturday night massacre and Elliot Richardson deciding to go a different way, then Attorney General of the United States. So because the American public's eyes are on all of us, I think it's important and as much as we can to be on our best behavior, but also to share with them some of the responsibilities that we have as a legislature, judiciary, and, of course, the executive.

So I'd be interested—I'm starting, first, with Mr. Miller's comments that were made over the weekend, Steve Miller, who indicated the executive power is all one singular and without any possibility of oversight or questioning. I think many of us took a step back, step to the side, and were either aghast or were trying to struggle with the Constitution or court precedent to find out what the basis of that was.

I'd appreciate your comment on that. And also appreciate the fact that the judiciary, likewise, does not have the authority to reach beyond its boundaries, to rule in a way that would skew the rights of the American people. They have—they interpret the law. And so I would love for you to, with this whole concept of transparency but also the judicial ethics as well, give the boundaries of the judiciary. And I'm, obviously, speaking about the Federal judiciary.

And then I'd appreciate as well that if American people—the American people, probably have not paid attention to the judiciary except for—let me not suggest that they're not engaged, but I was a judge in the municipal court, so except for their coming before municipal judges dealing with their citations or they may be in court for their own personal matters, now we've open the door for them to appreciate the value of this Nation.

What happens to their attitude about the courts and judges if—and I'm sure some of my colleagues raised this, if so-called judges, if he's a Mexican judge, so he has to be biassed? We are held together in this country by our adherence to the principles of our underpinning documents.

I yield to you, Mr. Geyh.

Mr. GEYH. This is a teaching moment. I think it—it is—the events, to me, had been troubling, but they offer an opportunity to talk to be people the way you describe. I think it's important to understand that—you know, earlier—earlier, I think it was Mr. Biggs who spoke, one spoke in terms of Marbury versus Madison being the first point at which judicial review was brought into the conversation.

But, in fact, it predated the formation of the Constitution. The judiciary has long been understood to have these powers to hold the other branches in check through the use of judicial review, through, you know, independent assessment of the law.

And when a member of the Administration stands up and says what the President says goes and implies that its power is absolute, I think it raises a flare for me, because it suggests that, first of all, that he doesn't understand the way the system works and that he is counting on people he is talking to not understanding the way the system works, and not understanding the judicial review is not just a bunch of people having second opinions.

They have a different role to play that—you know, throughout this conversation about whether the judges overreached in this scenario, I never once heard any discussion of the actual constitutional issues that were in play. This was all about judges overplaying their hand simply because they disagreed with the President. And I think this is a moment for all us to stop and say this is how the system works in very simple ways.

And honorable and men and women of integrity have a right to—not a right—have a duty to look at the law and decide how it goes. And you, in this room, have a right to criticize those decisions and say it is wrong during part of this public dialogue. But that stops short of saying: Because I disagree with you, you are illegitimate. Because I disagree with, you are someone who should be ignored or marginalized. And that is what worries me, that line between vigorous disagreement and delegitimization.

Ms. JACKSON LEE. Anyone else want to comment? Any anyone else?

All right. Let me thank—let me thank you very much. And might I, Mr. Chairman, just finish on this note. This is the body of people that will be dealing with these issues for a period of time, and I think this hearing, and to the Ranking Member, is a potent hearing, and I hope that as we go forward, we will understand that protecting these three branches of government is a bipartisan effort and we should strongly do so, as well as utilize our investigatory powers in ensuring the integrity of all aspects of government. And I hope we will be doing that for the American people.

I yield back. Thank you.

Mr. ISSA. I thank the gentlelady. I thank you for coming over and participating today. It was a welcome addition. I am going to try to close. Hopefully, I won't open any new wounds as I do it.

But, Professor Geyh, at the end, I detected something that I would like to not rebut but to add on to. You know, you talked about the executive branch feeling like, in national security, they had such broad powers as to not be questioned, and that is a debate that is not new. I have never seen a President who believed the War Powers Act actually affected them. The moment they get sworn in, it seems like that—you know, even if they were a former Member of this body, they move beyond that, so that is not uncommon.

But the court, the Ninth Circuit, does seem to have taken what it has been used to, and I live in the Ninth Circuit. It has been used to questioning the process of—in civil rights cases, of what intent is. So if—if somebody—if somebody's motives are not pure, then the law, even if perfectly written, is invalid in the Ninth Circuit. That is—they haven't been sustained very often when going to the Supreme Court, but they have had that view.

And in this case, it appears to me, as a bit of a layperson far removed, that they are doing the same thing in that they are determining that the President's statements and/or motives, in fact, are justification to overturn his ban not on the letter of it, not on the statute but, in fact, on his motives.

Would you agree that they have—they have taken that liberty, whether it is theirs or not, but they certainly indicated it.

Mr. GEYH. I have no opinion on that, but——

Mr. ISSA. You don't have an opinion on what the Ninth Circuit did?

Mr. GEYH. I don't—I have not studied the opinion in detail sufficient to draw that conclusion.

Mr. ISSA. You heard their words.

Mr. GEYH. But I don't disagree with you. I just have—I don't disagree with you. I am not challenging it. I am simply saying that I don't——

Mr. ISSA. Did either of you listen to the court review? Because I mean, I certainly heard it pretty loud and clear that they believe that they can judge the intent of the President in crafting something as invalidating it, regardless of the words. And I know that is not your subject expertise.

Mr. OSTERREICHER. If I may. I mean, at least in my listening to it, I think the court was trying to get evidence. I think they were listening to the government's side saying, no, this wasn't our intent, and then they looked toward the President's statements as being evidence of some intent. Whether or not that comes into play, as you said, in terms of the law versus the facts, obviously, we will see.

Mr. ISSA. And I do look forward to this, the case going to the court on—to the Supreme Court on that. Yes.

Mr. NADLER. Mr. Chairman, strike the last word. I would simply point out, first of all, the court, the—neither Judge Robart nor the Ninth Circuit decided the case. They were ruling on it on a temporary restraining order in which you don't go through all the evidence and make determinations, but you do say, well, who has a likelihood of prevailing on the merits, and as a matter of equity, who, in balancing the equities, who would be harmed if we let it stand or not stand. On that basis, the Ninth Circuit, I think, had ample reason to rule as it did because there had been no evidence showing harm if they overthrew it and plenty of evidence, obviously, the plaintiffs would be harmed if they didn't. I shouldn't say overthrown. Stay it.

And in terms of the constitutionality that you were referring to, they didn't make a finding. They couldn't until after the hearing, but they said there is a—not a possibility—likelihood of success on the merits, and they did look to intent there, which at this stage of the game they should.

Mr. ISSA. Well, and I am not in a position to agree or disagree. I was asking the question because the Ninth Circuit does look to intent. They have even overturned—they have overturned laws that were written in which a witness who came before the body that wrote the law, city council, the witness said something which they said went to intent. In other words, a tainted witness thus taints the decision of it. And it is—in looking at city council's laws, that may seem fairly benign, but in looking to a President who is entitled to, essentially, a right to privacy of his thoughts in deliberation and executive power, it will be interesting to see it before the Ninth Circuit.

I would like to quickly close—and I appreciate your input on that—and try to summarize what I think I have heard here today.

And, Mr. Osterreicher—I apologize. I have not gotten your name right once, but I have noticed it has been said several different ways.

Mr. OSTERREICHER. Just don't call me late for dinner.

Mr. ISSA. I think—I think the one thing, without calling you late for dinner, is that you have got agreement that there has been no showing that convinced anyone here at the dais that there is a reason not to video capture appellate activities broadly, which would potentially include the Supreme Court, but clearly would include all of the circuits. So I think you walked away today making your case for that. Obviously, I think it is fair to say there was less agreement as we got down to witnesses and victims and so on.

Professor Bruce, I think you made a compelling case. The only thing that I didn't hear was an oddity that is unique to this Member, and that is, that we have required the Administration, under the DATA Act, to put all information in machine-readable format. And one of the interesting things about PACER is, even if they handed you all the information, in order to make it usable to a broad public, it would have to be converted into machine readable with metadata attached. Isn't that true?

Mr. BRUCE. That is true. And frankly, I chose not to approach that issue today because I thought it was a bridge too far, but it is absolutely the case that it would need to be put into XML to be maximally used.

Mr. ISSA. Well, and I waited till the end to cover this because it is my intent to offer legislation that expands the DATA Act, which Senator Warner and I were the original authors of, to include Article III with the recognition that they have broad authority that does not happen to be one that is exclusive to them.

And so I will be offering that again with Senator Warner as a Senate companion for just that reason, that the bridge too far is, no matter what they do, the information they have is not currently as valuable as it should be.

Mr. BRUCE. That's correct. Thank you.

Mr. ISSA. And I think when it came to the questions of integrity of the court, although it was—there was a considerable discussion about the so-called judge comment, I think you made a compelling case here that it is a fragile court that even a 140-character statement by one individual, who happens to be the President of the United States, can have an effect on a court as can a question of whether this 80-year-old judge is competent, as is this judge biased, as is does the court system hold its own accountable, as is the question of whether or not there is a recognition of the financial holdings in some format of the—of members of the court as there are in the other two branches.

And so I think you made a good case that we will follow up on that we need to work with the court and/or work with our constitutional powers to add those so that no one can second-guess the court in those areas, which I think is a particularly important area, and I think you made a good case on it.

I would recognize Mr. Nadler if he had any other closing comments.

Mr. NADLER. No.

Mr. ISSA. Hearing none, I want to thank all of you. We will keep the record open for 5 days. If you have additional comments or thoughts afterwards, we would accept them into the record.

And with that, we stand adjourned.

[Whereupon, at 12:18 p.m., the Subcommittee was adjourned.]